MW00580395

I Want To Be A Nobody

God's Relentless Pursuit of Reluctant Leaders

Learn more about this book and its author by visiting our web site:

www.overboardministries.com

Copyright © 2018 Overboard Ministries

All rights reserved.

ISBN-10: 1-943635-19-6
ISBN-13:978-1-943635-19-1

Cover design by Keith Parker
Photo credit: Dan and Melissa Clark

This title is available for your favorite eReader. Visit
our web site to choose the format
that's right for you.

All comments or requests for
information should be sent to:
overboard@overboardministries.com

Unless otherwise noted, scripture quotations are taken from the
ENGLISH STANDARD VERSION. © 2001 by Crossway Bibles, a
division of Good News Publishers.

ENDORSEMENTS

Craig and Kori encourage me with their transparent stories of failure and insecurity. Page after page I thought, "Thank God I'm not the only one!" Even better, Craig and Kori don't leave us feeling sorry for them or for ourselves but explain how we can find our true selves in Jesus. Each chapter emphasizes this essential double truth: "I want to be a nobody"—well, you're in luck, because by yourself that's exactly what you are. "I want to be a nobody"—well, too bad, because you're in Christ, and you will forever be somebody in Him. So stop wishing you were somebody else and do what Jesus is calling you to do. Thanks, Craig and Kori. This is the straight, gospel-saturated pep talk I need.

Mike Wittmer
Professor of Systematic Theology
Grand Rapids Theological Seminary

* * * * *

Upon reading *I Want to be a Nobody* I could not help but think of the words of John the Baptist upon hearing the news of Jesus' growing popularity: "He must become greater; I must become less." Craig and Kori Trierweiler reflect this same spirit. Their gracious and humble reflections on leadership are a breath of fresh air, especially during a time when so many -- to their own demise -- clamor for the limelight of leadership.

I wholly commend this book. Read it, ponder it, and consider your own place among the unlikely people God delights to bring his love to a broken world.

Dr. Nick Twomey
Traverse City, Michigan

This Book is an encouraging word to all of us when we wonder if God was right when he called us into leadership. On those days when self-doubt, voices of accusation, and other critics clamor for your attention, this is the book to pick up. The encouragement that comes from Biblical leaders and Craig and Kori's personal lives will cause you to hear God's ongoing call and overcome self-doubt and second guessing. I have had the privilege of partnering with Craig and Kori and their Church in bringing the Gospel to Unreached people in India. In the process, I have been able to spend time with the Trierweilers and have been ministered to by their commitment to prayer, dependence on God's Word and clarity regarding God's call.

Todd Van Ek
President and CEO
Mission India

* * * * *

At last a book on leadership that doesn't leave us feeling that the bar is so high that we'll never measure up. Thanks to Craig and Kori's practical and biblical insights from the crucible of their own journey this book offers us hope for a more fruitful leadership experience in spite of those nagging insecurities that often rob us of the confidence to succeed. A must read for leaders who care about making a difference!

Dr. Joe Stowell
President
Cornerstone University

You feel like you're sitting in a room with two very candid and loving people as they talk back and forth to each other but also include you in the conversation. They understand and love. They are easy to read, vulnerable, candid, and very encouraging.

Whatever shortfalls you feel about yourself, you will find they have been there and understand, and you will be encouraged by the grace and strength of our Lord.

The Trierweilers -- don't try to pronounce it! -- take turns talking to each other and us about 14 reluctant leaders in the Bible. They show how God gave them remedy, and what that means for them as reluctant (but good, I add) leaders. And for us.

This should be for everybody! Listen in!

Knute Larson
Pastoral Coach and Teacher
Pastor Emeritus
The Chapel, Akron Ohio

* * * * *

As someone who has long been impeded by feelings of inadequacy, I appreciate Craig and Kori Trierweiler's biblical and very personal approach to dealing with the kinds of thoughts and feelings that paralyze many, if not most, Christians. The transparency found in *I Want to Be a Nobody!* gives an extra power surge to a book that left me filled with encouragement and depleted of excuses.

Gary Bower
Author
There's a Party in Heaven! and *The ABCs of God*

DEDICATION

This book is dedicated to Pastor David Standfest and Bob Boeve, two men who relentlessly pursue God and gave us two reluctant leaders, an opportunity to lead.

Thank you for your love of Jesus and wise leadership. Our lives are forever changed because of you!

CONTENTS

FOREWORD

As one who joyfully sits under Craig and Kori's leadership at
New Hope Community Church, I am grateful that they both
were willing to respond to God's call with the words, *"Here am I,
send me!"* Interestingly enough, as I read through this work, it
read a lot like my own autobiography. It reminded me of the
night God shook me to the core at a Christian camp.

As you read how Craig and Kori labor under the weight of their
call, those of us who benefit from their leadership don't
experience their fear or timidity, but rather boldness and an
unswerving commitment to sharing the truth of God's word,
without fear of reprisal. You get the sense that they would never
preach something that they have not first committed themselves
to live out.

Scripture declares, *"Consider your calling, brothers: not many of you
were wise according to worldly standards, not many were powerful,
not many were of noble birth. But God chose what is foolish in the
world to shame the wise" (1 Corinthians 1:26-27).* With candor and
vulnerability, Craig and Kori weave their own story through the
pages of Scripture to inspire all of us to make ourselves available
to the only one capable of doing *"exceedingly abundantly above all
we could ever ask or think.*

If you are wondering if you have the "goods" to make a
difference in someone else's world for Christ, this book is for
you! Unlike the self-help books that will seek to build up your
own sense of worth, for the Christian the greatest ability that we
offer to Christ is our availability.

As you read, *I Want to be a Nobody,* you will undoubtedly have
moments where you will want to push back and say, *"Yes,
but…"* Then as you continue to read there will likely be the
prompting of the Holy Spirit to submit your fears and doubts to
the only One who can take our inadequacy and use it to

confound the wise. Buckle up and be ready for the ride of your life. This book just may be the beginning of something very great, not only in your life but in the lives of those who experience the working of God through you.

Ken Riley
Executive Director
Lake Ann Camp

INTRODUCTION

"So, you want to be a nobody?" Those words from my wife hit me at the heart level and I immediately said, "It sounds like a book title." Kori and I were talking over dinner that Thursday evening at a local restaurant where we were recognized by several people who knew us because of our positional authority in the local church. As Senior Pastor, it is nearly impossible to blend in to the crowd or go unnoticed in public. Wherever we go we are always recognized, sometimes inspected, occasionally critiqued, and readily aware that we are under the microscope of opinions. Years ago (true story), we were 1,500 miles away from our home purchasing items from an orange grove in Florida when the cashier asked, "Do you know Craig Trierweiler?" With a backward hat and a smile, I admitted that I knew Craig very well.

On this particular evening out, as Kori and I sat there eating a plate of calamari, sipping a martini, and feeling self-conscious about being recognized by various people, I answered Kori, *"Yes, I want to be a nobody."* Leadership comes with a heavy mantle of responsibility, and there are many times leaders want to blend in with the crowd, escape it all, and simply be a nobody.

I don't think our experience is unique among followers of Jesus. As we examine both Scripture and human nature, it seems that whenever God calls people to lead, speak, or take a step of faith, our first response is almost always reluctance. We are reluctant because deep down we think when God called us, He made a mistake. When He chose us, He chose the wrong person. When He selected us, there were far better people. In other words, when God relentlessly pursues us, we are reluctant because we feel:

Unqualified. Uncertain. Unprepared. Untrained. Unwilling. Unlikely. Unforeseen. Unworthy. Unexpected. Unfit. Unclean. Unsatisfied. Uneducated. Undeserving.

Each of us face those 14 character dilemmas that challenge our emotions and make us feel like reluctant leaders. In this book, we have the privilege to speak to common human struggles, attempting to weave personal story and biblical reflection together in a way that navigates the challenges of leadership. Whether you are a business owner, church leader, parent, coworker, volunteer, or a member in the local church, each of these 14 traits hits at common heart issues.

The good news is that God doesn't make mistakes in His selection process. God doesn't call the qualified, but He qualifies those He calls. God doesn't choose the prepared, but He prepares those He chooses. God doesn't select those who are worthy, but He makes worthy those whom He selects. This is the radical good news of the gospel! He chooses the foolish, not the wise. He chooses the peasant, not the powerful. He chooses the weak, not the strong. He chooses the down-and-outer, not the up-and-comer. And God does it all so He gets the glory (see 1 Corinthians 1:26-31).

Kori and I never wanted to be leaders. As kids, we were more of followers and never aspired to be leaders. As Mike Berkley, product leader at Spotify, Viacom, and Comcast observes, *"Many leaders don't start out with the intention of becoming a leader...Many leaders fall into their leadership position as opposed to jumping into them."*[1] That was us. In God's providence, we found ourselves in the course of time falling into leadership, with positional authority and personal influence over many. This book explores God's relentless pursuit of reluctant leaders. The chapters are genuinely honest, painfully raw, slightly emotional, and perfectly candid as we encourage you in your own journey of reluctant leadership. Together, we must remember that we are all a bunch of nobodies who exist to make Somebody famous. And His name is Jesus!

Jeremiah 45:5
And do you seek great things for yourself? Seek them not.
(Baruch, the Scribe)

Chapter One
The Unqualified Leader: Moses
Craig Trierweiler

"Who am I that I should go to Pharaoh and bring the
children of Israel out of Egypt?"
Exodus 3:11

My Public Humiliation
It was a 1980s children's Christmas program at our local church.
Somewhere between 10 and 12 years old, I was one of the
headliners of the play, serving as a glorious shepherd who had
the simple task of declaring the great news of a Savior's birth.
My role and my speech were so critical to the birth of Jesus that
the technical crew had wired me up with a microphone. It
would be my first stage, my first public performance, and my
first debacle.

I blew my lines. I mean, this shepherd boy REALLY blew it. My
brain turned to a blank slate and I uttered meaningless nonsense
that drew looks of confusion from the cast and muttered
chuckles from the crowd. Totally embarrassed, I retreated
behind the makeshift stage where Mary, Joseph, wise men, and
other shepherds had gathered to celebrate their post-
performance excellence. High fives were given, congratulations
were extended to award-winning speeches. And then there was
me. My heart filled with shame and my face pouted with regret.
In pure anger, my internal rage burst through my lips: *"That*
sucked!"

My microphone was still on. And with that, my first public performance came to a screeching halt with public humiliation. I resolved then and there that I would never, ever speak again publicly. I was unqualified because of what I did and ashamed of who I was.

Moses, the Unqualified

David Brooks, in his op-ed article "The Reluctant Leader," notes that Moses is "the ultimate model for reluctant leadership."[2] After 400 years of bondage in Egypt, the Lord raised up a deliverer for His people. Moses was His chosen man. Born by a Hebrew woman, placed in a basket (literally, an "ark"), this boy would be the man God used to rescue Israel out of the grip of Egyptian slavery. But in Exodus chapters 3 and 4, when God called him at the burning bush experience, Moses had some fiery objections to God's choice of him as leader:

- **I am not qualified!**
  When the Lord says "I will send you," Moses immediately wonders, *"Who am I that I should go to Pharaoh and bring the children of Israel out of Egypt?" (Exodus 3:11)*. Who am I? It's a declaration of how Moses sees his personal value. "I'm not qualified! I don't have what it takes!" If God has ever called you to do anything significant, this is undoubtedly one of your first responses. "Who, me?"

  There are societal factors that have hounded me my entire life, making me feel unqualified to lead. As the youngest of three children, I never viewed myself as a leader. In fact, I was the follower, a tagalong. My personal assessment of self-worth has always been driven by feelings of weakness, instability, and being unqualified to do anything significant. Can you relate? "God, why me?" Even after two decades in ministry leadership, the feeling of being unqualified is still one of the primary obstacles to leadership. After working with leaders, I have come to realize that there is often a nagging sense of inadequacy attached to our lives that makes us question God's calling.

- **I am not acceptable!**
  Moses issues a second complaint to God: *"But, behold, they will not believe me or listen to my voice, for they will say, 'The Lord did not appear to you'" (Exodus 4:1).* Frankly, Moses doesn't want to look like an idiot. He doesn't want to take the stage on a public platform and blow his lines. He is concerned the people won't accept him and he will be left feeling the sting of rejection. He is saying, *"I don't have the skills and even if I did the people won't accept me."*

There are many skill factors that make me feel unacceptable as a leader. I am by nature a radical introvert, which basically means I like to be left alone. I like the corner chair in my home, not center stage at the church. I like the peace of a quiet room, not the noise of large crowds. I'm not an extrovert and I do not thrive when talking to masses of people. Oh, and I hate rejection. The very thing that Moses was concerned about is the thing that haunts me every day. I constantly wrestle with wanting to be accepted and the fear of being rejected.

I recall classes in high school where we were required to give five-minute speeches on issues ranging from the death penalty to civil rights. I was 15 or 16 years old, but those old memories of my failed "shepherd boy" speech still hounded me. I went to bed anxious the night before my speech and woke up nauseous the morning of, but I was forced to go to class. When it was my turn to speak, I felt the eyes of classmates piercing my soul and I heard the mocking voice inside my head cry out among the scoffers! Speaking was not my thing. Rejection is what I expected. And I was convinced that no matter what topic I would ever talk about, I would not be accepted by the people. Preparing for the speech, my heart raced and my palms were sweaty. During the speech, I fumbled for my words and felt the daunting stares of my classmates. After the speech, I felt like an unqualified loser. All of it reinforced those old shepherd boy failures that I was not acceptable. The fear of rejection is as common among leaders as a turkey at Thanksgiving. It is a core fear that makes us reluctant to obey God's calling.

- **I am not capable!**
Moses issues a third objection to God's choice of him as a leader: *"Oh, my Lord, I am not eloquent, either in the past or since you have spoken to your servant, but I am slow of speech and of tongue"* (Exodus 4:10). From a worldly perspective, there are things that are required to make one capable as a leader. One of the biggest requirements is an ability to speak with clarity and strength. And Moses knew he did not have that skill set. He stammered. He wasn't eloquent. He likely didn't want the public attention and was perfectly comfortable behind the scenes.

I wrestle with many fear factors that cause me to see myself as an incapable leader. When I consider the great orators of the day, I don't feel capable to do what God has called me to do. I don't like the public eye. I don't like public platforms. I have a healthy dose of glossophobia (fear of speaking in public). I like solitude and much of it is driven by an unsettling feeling that I am incapable of doing what God has called me to do. In my church office, a sign hangs above my window, quoting John Muir: *"The mountains are calling and I must go."* The quote beckons me to a place where leadership is not required, deadlines are not demanded, and phones are not ringing. And all of it is because I feel unqualified and incapable. One of the great obstacles that prevents people from taking risks is the internal fear of being exposed as a fraud.

- **I am not willing!**
  In Moses's final argument with God, he flat out protests: *"Oh, my Lord, please send someone else"* (Exodus 4:13). He felt so unqualified that he wanted God to choose someone else that had more political savvy than him. Perhaps he knew of his own wayward heart or his own sinful tendencies. Whatever it was, Moses was a reluctant leader who initially was unwilling to take the job.

When I look back on my life, I consider the number of sin factors that made me feel unqualified and wish God had chosen someone better to lead. In high school, I was a hypocritical teen who played both sides of the fence. When acting like a Christian, I was miserable because I felt like a fraud. When acting like the world, I was convicted because of my blatant hypocrisy. In my mid-teens, I got so drunk at a high school football game that I threw up and cleared an entire set of bleachers. In my first year of ministry at the church in 1999, I was the custodian responsible to clean toilets and mop floors. In my anger and frustration, I would throw trash cans, feeling that God had made a mistake calling me to such a lowly position. Even now, with all the pressures of managing church ministry, I recognize a temptation to self-medicate and evade the problems of life. All of it stems back to feeling incapable and unqualified. And the "Moses part of me" wishes God would choose someone else and leave me alone.

And yet, it turns out that God loves to use reluctant leaders who don't feel qualified, acceptable, capable, or willing. Perhaps it is people who reluctantly take the mantle of leadership who are the most qualified leaders in God's kingdom. After all, they are not in it for the glory, the praise, the authority, the position, or the honor. They are compelled to it by the inner work of God who has qualified them for the call.

Craig Trierweiler

Jesus, the True and Better Moses

So, here is Moses, protesting God's choice of him as the deliverer: *"I'm not qualified, I'm not acceptable, I'm not capable, and I'm not willing."* And then comes the birth of Jesus, who also was placed in a basket at his birth. His life, like Moses, was nearly cut off at infancy by those who wanted Him dead. He too would have a 40-day, 40-night experience with God in the wilderness. And like Moses, the Scripture is clear that Jesus did not have some external persona of angelic glory that would automatically draw people to His magnetic personality. Recall Isaiah who prophecies of Jesus:

> *"For he grew up before him like a young plant, and like a root out of dry ground; he had no form or majesty that we should look at him, and no beauty that we should desire him. He was despised and rejected by men; a man of sorrows, and acquainted with grief; and as one from whom men hide their faces he was despised, and we esteemed him not."* (Isaiah 53:2-3)

The Messiah would have no form or majesty that people would look at Him and be attracted to Him. In a human sense, it's why Moses protested being God's leader. Who would believe him? Who would accept him? Like Moses, this Messiah would be rejected and despised and acquainted with sorrows. This is why Moses tried to run from God's leadership demands. Moses did not want to be rejected!

Yet Jesus was the true and better Moses! I first heard that phrase, *"Jesus, True and Better,"* from a sermon by Tim Keller. Consider Jesus, who was the True and Better Moses:

- **Jesus was qualified.** He was qualified to deliver His people out of bondage and set us free. Being the radiance of the glory of God and making purification for sins, He became *"as much superior to angels as the name he has inherited is more excellent than theirs"* (Hebrews 1:3-4).

6

- **Jesus was acceptable.** His death and resurrection was a perfectly acceptable sacrifice, providing rescue for all who call on Him. It was such an acceptable work that Scripture promises if we sin, *"we have an advocate with the Father, Jesus Christ the righteous. He is the propitiation for our sins, and not for ours only but also for the sins of the whole world"* (1 John 2:1-2).

- **Jesus was capable.** When Jesus spoke, He did not stutter or stammer and lack eloquence. Being filled with the Spirit of power, the crowds *"were all amazed, so that they questioned among themselves, saying, 'What is this? A new teaching with authority!'"* (Mark 1:27).

- **Jesus was willing.** Whereas Moses was reluctant to accept his role of leadership, Jesus willingly "offered himself" without blemish to God (Hebrews 7:27 & 9:14). Speaking of His death, Jesus said, *"I lay down my life"* and *"No one takes it from me, but I lay it down of my own accord"* (John 10:17-18).

Reluctant Shepherd Boy, Then and Now

Remember that awkward moment when Craig the shepherd botched his lines and made an internal vow backstage that he would never speak again? Isn't it ironic that God would take that young man, call him to be a pastoral shepherd of a church, and push him onto a stage every Sunday with a microphone to speak God's word? I affirm to you that I am still the reluctant shepherd boy because I feel unqualified, unacceptable, incapable, and unwilling. I fear being rejected and that I'm not making a difference in peoples' lives. I am aware that there are people far more qualified than I am to shepherd God's people. And yet, because of God's call, this reluctant shepherd continues to speak. Not for my own glory. Not because of some personal desire to be successful. I shepherd and speak because God, in His wisdom, gently took a young man from the backstage and put him on the front stage to declare His truth. That's how God works. He loves to use nobodies to make much of Somebody!

Are you unqualified?

David Brooks continues in his article about reluctant leadership to give this news: *"The Bible is filled with reluctant leaders, people who did not choose power but were chosen for it...The Bible makes it clear that leadership is unpredictable: That the most powerful people often don't get to choose what they themselves will do."* And not only the Bible, but history has proven this as well. God chooses reluctant, unqualified leaders like Moses to accomplish His will.

- **You are qualified!** Colossians 1:12 says to give thanks to the Father because He has *"qualified you to share in the inheritance of the saints in light."* This is the very source of our qualification to lead! We are qualified, not because of ourselves, but because we have an awesome God who has qualified us in His son Jesus. No matter your view of self or number of times you've been humiliated publically, God looks for reluctant leaders who are willing to say yes to Him.

- **You are acceptable!** One of the great fears of obeying God is that we will make fools of ourselves. We don't want to take the stage, if you will, because we are convinced people will reject us. But, my friend, we have the greatest news in history—the resurrection of Jesus. And anyone who is raised from the dead has credibility! And for those of us in Jesus, we can be confident of knowing He accepts us, even if all others reject us.

- **You are capable!** Nearly everyone feels reluctant to lead because they don't feel eloquent or capable of speaking. Every Sunday I preach, the anxiety and butterflies fill my stomach because I recognize I am not capable to do what God has called me to do. But then I realize, "I am not alone! I have the Holy Spirit in me who has promised to empower me to do His will." So, just before I take the stage, this reluctant leader bows his head and prays Proverbs 21:31: *"Lord, the horse is prepared for battle, but you give the victory."* It's a strange Proverb, but what it means is, *"Lord, I've done all I can do in preparation and study, but now I look to you as the one capable to use my voice to make a difference in the lives of people."*

- **You are willing!** God is looking for willing and obedient hearts. Too many people in history have abdicated their responsibility to others. My friend, from of old, God has given His people a choice of life or death. Life, if you obey. Death, if you disobey. It is perfectly understandable that our initial response to God's call is reluctance because of the risks involved. But God is looking for people like Moses who will yield to Him in spite of all the objections, and serve Him with a willing spirit.

Kori's Response

I think Moses and I would be good friends. I so identify with being afraid to speak up. Keeping my mouth shut is my "go to" in an uncomfortable situation. My uncle used to say, "It's better to keep your mouth shut and let everyone assume you're an idiot, than to open your mouth and remove all doubt." But when God calls us, like Moses, to go and speak, that isn't an option. The promise I cling to is the word God spoke to Moses, *"Now therefore go, and I will be with your mouth and teach you what you shall speak"* (Exodus 4:12). I am glad Moses, the unqualified leader, gave proof of God's promise when he was obedient to the call. I look forward to meeting him in glory someday as a fellow unqualified leader!

Chapter Two
The Uncertain Leader: Joshua
Kori Trierweiler

"Just as I was with Moses, so I will be with you. I will not leave your or forsake you."
Joshua 1: 5

She was a legend. A superstar. The one who had been there since the very beginning. She had multiple degrees, great people skills, not to mention a deep love and concern for the ladies of our community. She was the founder of the Women's Ministry team at our church and had held that position for many years. She was amazing at the job, but now she had decided to step out of that role.

I had been on her team for less than a year, the youngest of them all, when she and the Senior Pastor asked if I would take over the role of Women's Ministry Director. What!? Me? No! Being one the pastors' wives of the church, it might've seemed like the right call, but I was NOT at all certain. I had four young kids at home. I preferred one-on-one interaction to large crowds, was scared to death of public speaking, and could barely keep my house clean (not that that one is a requirement for the role but it sure did seem like my chronically messy house spoke loud accusations of failure to me). Besides, I liked my safe and comfortable position as "one of the team members" and didn't really see myself as the "natural-born-leader" type. So when the opportunity came for me to take the position of leadership, I was super reluctant to even consider the role.

Joshua, the Uncertain

Joshua was up to bat. Moses, their leader, his mentor, ally, and friend was gone. The Israelites had large portions of land to conquer and they were all looking to Joshua as their new leader to make it happen. All eyes were on him to get this right. No doubt he was being compared by some to the way Moses used to do things, and perhaps there were some who wondered if he had what it took. Can Joshua really take a group of people that have never experienced combat, train them, and lead them through victorious battles to claim their land? No doubt the people murmured, doubted, and their anxieties fed and accelerated his own. Perhaps his greatest enemy wasn't the hostile nations but rather his own fear and intimidation. It's amazing how uncertainty and self-doubt can rob you of clarity of thought and paralyze you from taking any form of action at all. And yet, here it is...the promise from God:

> "Just as I was with Moses, so I will be with you. I will not leave you or forsake you. Be strong and courageous, for you shall cause this people to inherit the land that I swore to their fathers to give them. Only be strong and very courageous, being careful to do according to all the law that Moses my servant commanded you." (Joshua 1: 5-7)

After much prayer, I accepted the role of Women's Ministry Director and was excited to see what God had in store for the beautiful ladies of our church. I had ideas rolling around in my head, and I wanted to get alone with God to seek His guidance and make plans for the next year of ministry. I wanted to get it on the calendar so that my team and I could start making it happen. I HAD to because, as the new director, it was up to me to create amazing spiritual growth opportunities, loaded with inspiring events large amounts of women would come to and walk away from with awesome encounters with God. This would prove my excellent leadership capabilities. It's amazing how much need for approval can be packed into one little job title.

I got a babysitter, cleared my morning, and got alone with God with an open Bible and an empty notebook to put together THE PLAN for the year. I was so excited and ready to fill that notebook to the brim with His amazing instructions. But when I got quiet enough to listen to His still, small voice, I only heard one thing.

Kori, do nothing but pray for a year.

Wow, not what I was expecting. But the message came over and over that morning loud and clear. I was to plan nothing, start nothing, cease from activities, and do nothing but pray for an entire ministry season (September-May). "Is that even allowed?" I thought. *God, are you sure these are your instructions? You never told the last women's ministry team to do this. These seem like risky instructions and a lot of inactivity. How are we ever going to get any work done? Will prayer really accomplish everything I hope and dream for my sisters at New Hope Church?*

I take comfort in the fact that I am not the only one to get unusual instructions as a brand new leader. In one of Joshua's first big "make it or break it" military battles, he too receives crazy instructions from the Lord. He was ordered to take his men and march around the city of Jericho once every day for six days in silence, and then on the seventh day, switch it up a bit by marching around the city of Jericho seven times. And for the grand finale, the men were to shout while the priests blew trumpets. That's it! No further instructions or guarantees except the promise that God had already given them the city.

My instructions as the new director were to do nothing but pray for a year. So with a bit of uncertainty, I gathered my faithful "roll up your sleeves and get started" team to let them know what I thought I was hearing from the Lord. *What if they all think I am crazy? Totally off base? What if they shake their heads and agree*

13

that I am just too young and obviously not the right lady for the job? Or what if I try to lead with this idea and they flat out refuse to follow me? "Lord," I prayed, "if this is You directing me, then You have to make a way for this." I only saw two options: I trust God and He comes through for me or I fall flat on my face.

I am humbled to tell you that when I explained the "plan" to the ladies, they wholeheartedly agreed. We began meeting on a regular basis and spending hours of time in prayer, pouring our hearts out to the Lord for the women of our church.

We felt led to keep one ongoing ladies event that met once a month, but other than that, our women's ministry was pretty dormant. So many times I was tempted to do something, plan something, make something/anything happen, but was always led to wait. There were times ladies would ask me about women's ministry events in the church and I would question myself all over again. I would quickly tell them all about our one monthly event, while fear and self-doubt would creep into my thinking. *What if I'm totally failing these ladies by not providing various Bible studies, scouting out speaking conferences to attend, or creating and promoting personal retreats for them? I am the worst WM Director ever!* Then I would be reminded of our powerful, Holy Spirit-drenched prayer times for these dear women and the love that God was giving me for them, and His peace would come to me. **Do nothing but pray this year.**

Against all the fears and "what ifs," Joshua faithfully followed the Lord's instructions. Just think about this: Day 1: March around the city in silence and then go back to camp. Day 2: Repeat day 1. Day 3: Repeat. Day 4: Repeat. Day 5: Repeat. Day 6: Repeat. Maybe the men were beginning to get restless from having to stay silent, while casually walking around the city and then sitting around camp waiting for something to happen. For Joshua, that's a lot of downtime for doubts and second guessing of the plan to flood in. And yet, there was the promise...*Be careful to do all that I commanded you, Be strong and Courageous.*

We know how Joshua's battle ended with a miraculous work of God. The huge, impenetrable walls of Jericho literally fell down, leaving the enemy exposed. The Israelites claimed a huge victory that is still talked about today. It was the beginning of many victories to come and it elevated Joshua to the mighty warrior and man of faith we all know him as. He had to listen and follow the unconventional instructions of God instead of the normal military protocol of that day. The uncertain leader had to choose faith in God's word over fear of failure.

Maybe at this time you expect me to tell you of this amazing victory that resulted from our year of inactivity and unseen meetings of prayer. But let me tell you what happened next. At the close of the year, our Senior Pastor made an announcement of his desire to get a Women's Ministry Program up and running at our church. He asked any ladies who were interested to come to a meeting after service. He was going to put together a leadership team that would "jump start this much needed ministry and hit the ground running." This announcement hit all my fears and uncertainties. All my previous thoughts that I was failing the ladies of our church came rushing at me and threatened to drown me right there, until I heard and felt the Lord's presence so very close to me. He came in and enveloped me in a God-hug and said, *"You have not failed Me. You have done everything I have asked you to do, My child."*

You see, it was God's plan all along to assign me the leadership of this ministry for that year—the year of prayer. I was the director for that season because it was a season for sowing seeds of prayer, a massive planting of desires and dreams for the ladies that God would take, hold, and harvest for each woman at the proper time. I didn't have that perspective coming into the job, but I'm glad I do now. I assumed my role would look similar to the former Women's Ministry Director. But I wasn't like her, and I wasn't going to be like the next leader either. All of us were needed to accomplish His will at the right time for His ministry. We belong to Him and get our instructions from Him.

So like the battle of Jericho, was there a massive victory fought and won that year when God told us to do nothing but pray? Did impenetrable walls fall down? Was the enemy defeated? Perhaps there were requests we made that are still being answered by God to this day. What about the deep, heart-level victories we might never know about? How about all the times God granted freedom from fears, brought about salvation, granted forgiveness, mended relationships, overcame infertility, provided supernatural help at just the right time, or rescued woman in the midst of dark temptation? I know that from the outside looking in, my year as the director may have looked like a total flop. Some might even say it was a waste of time and a disservice to the ministry. I cannot tell you for sure, but I do know the record books in eternity will tell the tales. I guess the MOST important question is: Jesus, did I complete the work You gave me to do?

Like Joshua, we don't have to have all the answers. We don't have to be like the leaders who have gone before us or the ones who come after us. We only need to hear and obey when it's our turn to take the lead, trusting that God has equipped us for the right task and the right time. Joshua didn't have to be like Moses. With all his uncertainty, all Joshua needed was to be the leader God wanted him to be. And that, I believe he learned a long time ago in the tent of meeting: *"Thus the Lord used to speak to Moses face to face, as a man speaks to his friend. When Moses turned again into the camp, his assistant Joshua the son of Nun, a young man, would not depart from the tent"* (Exodus 33:11).

The tent of meeting was the place Moses went to get instructions from the Lord for the people of Israel. Joshua, being Moses's right-hand man naturally went with him, learning to walk like he did. But it is interesting that even when Moses was done meeting with the Lord, Joshua stayed behind. He lingered alone in the presence of God. The tent of meeting is where the presence of the Lord dwelt. It was there that Joshua learned, not how to be like Moses, but how to receive and obey instructions from God.

Jesus, the True and Better Joshua

Just as Joshua spent large amounts of time in the tent of meeting, soaking up God's presence, receiving instructions, and gaining the power to obey them, there is One even better than him who did that continually and perfectly—Jesus. He was careful to retreat to quiet places and get alone with His Father to receive instructions from Him. This is what He said: *"I can do nothing on my own. As I hear, I judge, and my judgment is just, because I seek not my own will but the will of him who sent me"* (John 5:30).

When Jesus walked this earth, He was in continual communication with His Father by the power of the Holy Spirit. He was always listening for His Father's detailed directions in order to obey everything. The Amplified version puts it this way: *"As the voice comes to Me, so I give a decision."* Jesus is the true and better Joshua, who spent time with God and was careful to listen and obey every instruction He was given. Just like Joshua, Jesus led the attack on the enemy that supernaturally caused the walls of the kingdom of darkness to fall. As a result, you and I can join Him in the battle to claim the victory! Just like the Israelites, we enter the land of abundance that is the inheritance of Christ, our very own Kingdom of Heaven.

My year as the Director of Women's Ministries taught me we don't always know what victory is going to look like. But in Christ we are more than conquerors. Abiding with Jesus, spending time with Him, listening for His instructions, He leads us from victory to victory!

Craig's Response

I can identify with the fear and uncertainty of taking over leadership from men who are highly revered. Our founding pastor, David Standfest, was a strong visionary leader whose faith could move mountains. He passed the baton to Bob Boeve for two years, who administered leadership and administration with precision and excellence. When I received the baton of leadership at 35 years old, I felt like Solomon—"young and inexperienced." And when you feel that way, it leads to uncertainty as a leader.

I take great comfort in what Hebrews 11 says about Abraham's walk of faith. When God called him to obey, it says that Abraham went "going, not knowing where he was going." That is Joshua's story. That is our story. Ordinary people who are called by an extraordinary God to obey even when it doesn't make sense. The walk of faith requires an element of uncertainty on our part, but at the core we are absolutely certain in the power of God who is leading us. If you are at a place where God is calling you to go, not knowing where you are going, welcome to the realm of uncertain leadership!

Chapter Three
The Unprepared Leader: Samuel
Craig Trierweiler

"Go, lie down, and if he calls you, you shall say
'Speak, Lord, for your servant hears.'"
1 Samuel 3:9

My Calling to Ministry
It was a cold winter night in February 1994. I was 16 years old and at a proverbial crossroads. I had my pursuits, plans, and dreams, and none of them were guided by prayer or the leading of the Holy Spirit.

At that time in life, I had never "heard" the voice of the Lord. When I say "heard" I don't mean an audible voice in my head. I simply mean that I had never heard the clear leading of the Holy Spirit Who speaks a personal word in your heart. On this night, I would hear the Lord for the first time, and it would forever change the direction of my life.

It was nearly midnight at a youth retreat at Lake Ann Camp. I was sitting alone in the snow, leaning against a lamppost, the light above me shining on the pages of my Bible. I was reading the book of Philippians where Paul writes about all his pursuits without the Lord and the credentials he had accumulated in his own flesh. But then he makes a profound statement: *"Whatever*

19

was to my profit, I now consider loss for the sake of Christ" (Philippians 3:7).

In the business world, it's a P&L statement (Profit & Loss). The next seven verses would begin to shape the clear voice of God in my inner being. The things Paul once considered profit—every single one of them—he now considered loss, rubbish, or garbage if only he could know Jesus Christ. In other words, if Jesus was the only thing on the "Profit" side of the spreadsheet, then everything else in life would still be considered "Loss" to him. From that moment, Paul's life was changed because of the all-surpassing profit of knowing Jesus. Then I read these words, which caused the light of heaven to flood down upon my heart: *"I press on to take hold of that for which Christ Jesus took hold of me"* (Philippians 3:12).

I still remember the clear, inner voice of the Holy Spirit: **"Craig, I'm calling you to ministry."** That was it. No angelic announcement. No shooting stars zooming in the sky. No weird message burned into the snow. Just the Word of God combined with the Spirit of God Who spoke a clear testimony. And for the first time in my life, I heard the voice of God.

But here is the deal. I was totally unprepared for what He was calling me to do! I was the youngest in my family. The goofball in my school. The hypocrite in my youth group. The unqualified shepherd boy who publicly humiliated himself on stage. God was calling me, but I was unprepared and scared. But, when God speaks and calls you to something, He is looking for what a pastor friend of mine, Nick Twomey refers to as IRCO: instant, radical, and costly obedience.

Samuel, the Unprepared
The Scripture has a story about a young man named Samuel whose mom had dealt with infertility for years. Begging God for a child, she vowed that if God gave her a son, she would *"give him to the Lord all the days of his life"* (1 Samuel 1:11). In other words, her son would be dedicated to the work of what we

would consider pastoral ministry. This boy would be a minister of God's word to the people.

In the course of time, God did bless Hannah with a son, whom she named Samuel. And in time, she fulfilled her vow and dedicated Samuel to minister at the house of God. He had no training or credentials. Samuel was simply an understudy, an intern who was learning the ropes of ministry leadership. Unfortunately, his mentors were all bad examples. Eli, the priest, was old, unwise, and passive in his leadership. And Eli's two grown sons, who were in charge of the sacrifices and offerings, were disobedient, rebellious, and prone to sexual misconduct with women who came to worship. At this point, Samuel was young, inexperienced, and totally unprepared for leadership.

The Preparation of a Leader
The good news is that God does not call the prepared, but rather prepares those He calls. As God called Samuel to a position of leadership, He also prepared the young man to accomplish what He was calling him to do. As Samuel began to respond to the work God called him to, he did three specific things which helped prepare him for ministry:

- **Proximity to the Presence of God.**
  The tabernacle was the one place where heaven and earth met. It was the place of God's presence on earth. It was where people would come to encounter the God of creation. One night while Eli the priest had gone home to bed, young Samuel was *"lying down in the temple of the Lord, where the ark of God was"* (1 Samuel 3:3). As of yet, Samuel had not heard the voice of God. But notice where he parked himself. Even at night, he situated himself as close as he could to the presence of God. In the words of an old book by Brother Lawrence, he was "practicing the presence of God."[3]

  I heard a story of a young girl in our church who struggles with fear and anxiety at night. To combat the

21

fear, one thing that brings her comfort is to sleep with her Bible under her pillow. There's something comforting about knowing that you are dwelling in the presence of God!

Nothing can prepare a person more for leadership and life than proximity to the presence of God. Jesus would later call it *abiding*. I believe that churches across our country are being led by people who are not in close proximity to the presence of God. Many pastors step into pulpits with their own eloquence or charm, but they are unprepared leaders who have not heard from the Lord or prepared their heart in His presence. The prophet Jeremiah warns of such unprepared spiritual leaders: *"I did not send the prophets, yet they ran; I did not speak to them, yet they prophesied. But if they had stood in my council, then they would have proclaimed my words to my people"* (Jeremiah 23:21-22).

Imagine it! Sunday after Sunday, men of God stand in the pulpit for 45 minutes, but have not stood in the presence of God for 45 seconds all week! The preparation of a leader begins with a person's proximity to the presence of God. And that is where young Samuel begins —sleeping where the ark of God was.

- **Attention to the Voice of God.**
At 16 years old, I heard the voice of God for the first time. I was not well trained in hearing the Lord, but when He spoke it was unmistakable. In our day, hearing God's voice comes through His Word, by His Spirit. The Word and the Spirit always work in tandem. In Samuel's day, the *"word of the Lord was rare"* (1 Samuel 3:1), but it was not uncommon for the Lord to speak directly to a prophet with clarity and conviction.

We see in the story that as Samuel lay sleeping next to the ark, he heard his name called. (By the way, Samuel's name means *"heard of God."*) The repetition of God calling Samuel is almost comical as Samuel doesn't quite know what to do or how to respond.

"The Lord called Samuel" (v. 4).

"The Lord called again, 'Samuel!'" (v. 6).

"The Lord called Samuel again the third time" (v. 8).

"The Lord came and stood, calling as at other times, 'Samuel, Samuel!'" (v. 10).

Aren't you glad that God doesn't give up after He calls us the first time? When you are an unprepared leader, it takes time to discern the voice of God. Like me at 16 years old, Samuel was learning to be attentive to the voice of the Lord, but still needed discernment.

At my current stage of life, my second daughter is beginning to drive and is learning to be attentive to the voice of her instructor. Our state requires 50 hours of drive time that is mentored by a seasoned driver. Of that required time, 10 hours must be from driving at night. The whole point of monitored drive time is that a person learns to navigate a vehicle, with the voice of an instructor, under various conditions, until they themselves can operate alone. One of my daughter's driving instructors used to say that *"being a driving instructor is hours of boredom followed by your life suddenly flashing before your eyes."* Indeed. In the same way, Samuel is being prepared as a leader and it all starts with discerning the voice of the Instructor.

Samuel is an unprepared leader who must learn to discern God's voice. Being unfamiliar with the voice of God, young Samuel would wake from his sleep and immediately rush out to see Eli, thinking the priest was calling. Again, the repetition is almost comical:

"Here I am, for you called me" (v. 5).

"Here I am, for you called me" (v. 6).

"Here I am, for you called me" (v. 8).

Every parent knows what it's like to have a child wake them during night hours. Sometimes they need to use the bathroom. Sometimes they are scared. Sometimes they had a bad dream. Imagine Eli's frustration when four times in the middle of his sleep, a young intern rushes in to wake him up! Eli does what we all would do in this situation: *"Lie down! Lie down! Lie down!"* But, finally even Eli realizes God may be working in Samuel's life: *"Go, lie down, and if he calls you, you shall say 'Speak, Lord, for your servant hears'"* (v. 9).

How well have we learned to hear God's voice? Here is an admission. After I heard God clearly call me into ministry, I eventually went to Bible school. At that time, I was unqualified and unprepared for ministry. Bible school and seminary were invaluable, teaching me many things about theology and ministry practices. But I can say almost unequivocally, Bible school did very little when it came to being attentive to the voice of God. School may teach you how to pastor, but it does little to teach you how to pray. It may teach you how to read Greek, but it doesn't teach you how to hear God speak. It may teach you how to craft a sermon, but it doesn't teach you how to abide in God's presence. Bible school is invaluable to learn how to study the Scripture. But it is very possible to come out intellectually brilliant, yet spiritually anemic. As a result, many ministers are in charge of churches who lead like Eli's sons, without God's blessing.

- **Obedience to the Will of God.**
  The fourth time Samuel heard his name, he responded: *"Speak, for your servant hears"* (v. 10). This would prove to be the turning point of Samuel's life. From here on, God would be preparing an unprepared man to be used mightily in the land of Israel. Samuel was growing and discerning God's voice, and as a result, *"Samuel grew, and*

the Lord was with him and let none of his words fall to ground" (1 Samuel 3:19).

Whatever else we learn from Samuel, may we learn his posture of hearing the voice of God. What if every time we read the Scripture, we simply bowed our head and said, *"Speak, Lord, for your servant hears"*? What if every Sunday before the word is preached, we bowed our head and said, *"Speak, Lord, for your servant hears"*? God is not impressed by thesis papers, seminary degrees, or even intellectual knowledge. God is impressed by people like Samuel who have proximity to the presence of God, give attention to the voice of God, and display obedience to the will of God.

Jesus, the True and Better Samuel

When Jesus was a young boy like Samuel, the same thing was true of Him. Luke 2 tells us that Jesus *"grew and became strong, filled with wisdom. And the favor of God was upon him"* (v. 40). The narrative of Jesus is strikingly similar to that of Samuel, except Jesus is the true and better Samuel in every respect!

• **Proximity to the Presence of God.** In the famous passage where Jesus was 12 years old and separated from His parents for three days, notice where was He eventually found: in His Father's house! It's just like Samuel who slept in the presence of the Almighty. From an early age, it was clear that Jesus prioritized proximity to the presence of His Father, even saying to His mother, *"Did you not know that I MUST be in my Father's house?"* (v. 49). In reading the gospels, it is evident that Jesus had a pattern of spending time with His Father. In places like Luke 5:16, it says that Jesus *"would withdraw to desolate places and pray."* He was practicing the presence of God. From the very start of His ministry, His preparation for leadership began with spending time in God's presence. We cannot give to our people what we do not possess.

25

- **Attention to the Voice of God.** Just before Jesus raised Lazarus from the dead, He lifted up His voice in prayer so everyone could hear: *"Father, I thank you that you have heard me. I knew that you always hear me, but I said this on account of the people standing around, that they may believe that you sent me"* (John 11:41-42). His preparation for ministry came from attention to the voice of His Father. As I recall the days of Bible school, there was not one class that taught us to pray. They taught us doctrine, church history, pastoral management, and other details of running the church. But not once was there instruction on how to pray or lead your people to pay attention to the voice of God. My friends, if our churches are to make a difference in our culture, they must be led by men who pray and pay attention to the voice of God.

- **Obedience to the Will of God.** Remember what it said of Samuel? *"The Lord was with him and let none of his words fall to the ground"* (1 Samuel 3:19). Samuel was obedient and as a result the Lord took an unprepared young man and made him an accomplished leader. With Jesus, the eternal Son, we find complete, perfect obedience to His Father's will. In John 17:4 Jesus prays, *"I glorified you on earth, having accomplished the work that you gave me to do."* None of us obeys God perfectly, and yet Jesus accomplished everything His Father called Him to do. He is the true and better Samuel whose obedience to the Father was done to perfection.

Position Does not Guarantee Preparation

Since 1999, I have served at New Hope Community Church starting as a janitor, and transitioning through various positions including roles in small groups, education, administration, teaching pastor, and eventually Senior Pastor. Here's what I can tell you: Positional power does not automatically mean one is prepared to lead. Position does not mean one has been in proximity to God. The apostle Paul talks about the *"daily pressure on me of my anxiety for all the churches"* (2 Corinthians

11:28). Anyone in a position of leadership knows that these pressures can sap the life and vitality out of ministry. Eli did not exercise spiritual leadership from a close proximity to the Lord. His sons did not exercise spiritual leadership by being attentive to the voice of God. In spite of their positions, those men were unprepared leaders whose influence did more harm than good.

So, what did God do? He found an unprepared boy to do His work. He found a boy who prioritizes proximity to His presence, pays attention to His voice, and obeys His will. Those are the type of leaders God is looking to use. You may feel unqualified and unprepared to be used by God, but in God's economy, the people who are most used are those who often feel the least prepared.

I have always felt unprepared to do God's work. One of those seasons was around 2006 where I was put on probation for lack of effort and was on the brink of losing my job. I had nowhere else to go and nobody to turn to except the Lord. About midnight during that season, I took my Bible and drove my car to a local grocery store where I once again sat under a streetlight. It was there that God's Spirit used God's Word to shine light into my heart. It was in Psalm 78:70-72:
> "He chose David his servant and took him from the sheepfolds; from following the nursing ewes he brought him to shepherd Jacob his people, Israel his inheritance. With upright heart he shepherded them and guided them with his skillful hand."

Just like when I was 16, God met me again with His still small voice. Simply put, He reassured me that He was doing a hidden work in my life and was using my season of pain to prepare me as a shepherd of His people! God was preparing an unprepared man and giving him hope of being used in the future. When I heard God's voice, I was humbled and wept with gratitude!

So What About You?
- **Proximity to the Presence of God.** God's preparation of a leader begins with how well a person prioritizes

proximity to His presence. How well do you prioritize proximity to God's presence? Do you sleep next to the ark of God? Do you make a daily habit of abiding in the presence of the Lord? These are fundamental habits that prepare you for being used by God.

- **Attention to the Voice of God.** Becoming prepared requires that we pay attention to the voice of God. How often do you pray and submit yourself to hearing the voice of God through His Word? Consider making it a daily habit to say along with Samuel, *"Speak, Lord, for your servant hears."*

- **Obedience to the Will of God.** Are you walking in obedience to the Lord? Are there works He has called you to do? You may have position, power, and influence. So do I. But when the Lord looks at your life, does He see a man or woman who walks with integrity and responds with obedience?

Kori's Response
I remember as a young girl overhearing my mom say, "Jesus gets sweeter and sweeter each day." For some reason that sentence got stuck in my head and for the next few days it kept coming back to me. My young mind began to ponder what in the world my mom could be talking about. With those thoughts came a desire to know who Jesus is and what she meant by Him getting sweeter by the day. I began to plan how I could get up earlier each morning to read the Bible and talk with Jesus. What I didn't know then was that those ideas were the whisper of the Holy Spirit, taking what my mom had said to plant desire and action that moved me toward Jesus. Like young Samuel, the unprepared leader, I am glad you don't have to be a certain age to be trained by the voice of God. Morning after morning, as I met with the Lord, read His word and talked through my day with Him, little did I know that He was preparing me for future works.

Chapter Four
The Unlikely Leader: David
Kori Trierweiler

"Then Samuel said to Jesse, 'Are all your sons here?'
And he said, 'There remains yet the youngest,
but behold, he is keeping the sheep.'
And Samuel said to Jesse, 'Send and get him,
for we will not sit down till he comes here.'"
1 Samuel 16:11

Oh no! What did I just get myself into? Is this really happening? And most importantly, is it too late to back out of this? These were my thoughts on the drive home from the planning committee meeting.

About five years after my role as director of Women's Ministries, the Lord began talking to me about an idea He had. It was a new assignment. It started as a whispered suggestion in my quiet time with the Lord and grew from there. His idea terrified me at first and, I have to be honest, I ignored it for a while. God hinted that He wanted me to be His spokeswoman and He wanted to use me to teach the word of God to women. To date, my only public speaking experience was speech class in college where I was forced to fill a 20-minute time slot in front of a group of classmates. All I remember was that I spent five minutes slowly handing out papers just to fill my time quota. Although I did pass the class, not surprisingly, I didn't score very high and my professor certainly wasn't recommending me for a career in public speaking.

Now, back to my panic moment in the car. The week before the planning meeting was to take place I began to experience something new. Throughout the day my mind was flooded with all kinds of thoughts, ideas, passages of Scripture, and personal stories about prayer. It was as if I was being prepared for something. The next day I was having thoughts about the Holy Spirit. It was like my mind was putting together an outline of a lesson. *Jesus, what is this? It feels new and different, urgent even, like I have a message and it has to be shared with someone soon!*

As soon as I asked that, my next thought settled on the upcoming prayer retreat, and I strongly sensed that the Lord wanted me to speak at the retreat. *Oh no, not going to happen. Even if I wanted to (which I don't) they wouldn't ask me. I've never taught a lesson or delivered a message of any kind before.*

On the way to the gathering, I remember having a talk with God about His suggestion that I would be the speaker at this event. I told Him that if He wanted me to do it, He would have to make it undeniably clear because I certainly wasn't going to volunteer for it! I arrived at the place and settled in with coffee before the planning meeting was called to order. The leader worked through every aspect of what was needed to pull off this event. Cost, selling of tickets, venue, meals, activities, and then she arrived at the topic of who would be the key speaker for the weekend. It was an open discussion. I sealed my lips and held my breath, fully expecting to hear lots of ideas on a guest we could bring in to make this weekend a smashing success. But instead, there was a long pause. The room went silent...all except for the pounding of my heart. And then she casually said, "Would any of you like to speak at this event?"

What did she just say? Did I hear her correctly? Why would she ask that? Then I heard His voice, **Kori, you know why she said that. I am making a way for you. Speak up. It's now or never.**

The next thing I heard was my voice speaking (without my consent) saying timidly, "I might have a few things to say, maybe?"

"Ok," she said. "What would you want to talk about?"

"Prayer and the Holy Spirit," I answered.

I watched her nod her head, write them down, and move on to the next subject. She acted like that area of the retreat was completely taken care of and we were now wrapping up the meeting. My mind went blank and my heart raced in fear. I remember several minutes later literally stopping the meeting to explain to these ladies how unqualified and unlikely of a candidate I was to speak at this event. I told them that I have never spoken at any event like this before and I wasn't even sure I could. My fear was that I could very possibly ruin everything! The ladies reassured me and stopped to pray for me, but they wisely held me to the commitment. As I drove home, I couldn't help but think, "Oh no, what did I just get myself into?"

David, the Unlikely Leader
I'll do it. I'll fight that giant. That's what David, even as a young boy, decided to do. How did he do it? How did he have the courage to face the giant when seasoned warriors were too afraid? Why was David ready to fight Goliath after hearing his mocking only one time, when the Israelite army had heard him day after day? Could it be that the glory of God was more important to David than the fear of death?

Before visiting the Israelite camp, David had spent the majority of his time in the presence of the Lord, alone, tending the sheep. Singing, playing his harp, throwing rocks from his sling, enjoying the solitude, all the while praising God and spending time with Him each day. Meanwhile, the men of Israel were being beaten down, listening to the taunts of the enemy and their own inability to do anything about it. The words of the enemy were drenched in fear and had weighed heavily on the minds and hearts of the Israelite warriors. But David wasn't trained in the military camp with the other men. David was trained in secret.

David knew what it was like to be with the Lord God Almighty. He was jealous for His glory and took great offense at what Goliath was saying against his God, his helper, his friend! How dare Goliath! That was the attitude David had towards the giant. Why? What did David have the rest of them didn't? Simply put, David had a deep, personal encounter with the Lord. David KNEW God. How? He spent many hours alone with Him as a shepherd in the fields. He felt God, and the Lord built up many mighty experiences with David. Even though David was young, he had a history with God, and God had a plan for him. Even though he was the most unlikely choice out of all his brothers, God wanted this young shepherd boy to be a leader, the next king of His people.

So God sent the prophet Samuel to Jesse's house to anoint a new king, but the unlikely David wasn't even invited to the gathering. Samuel took a look at each of Jesse's sons, inquiring of the Lord, while sizing up the strong, strapping brothers that filled the room. From the eldest to the second born, third born, and down the line, God kept saying, "No, not this one." Bewildered, Samuel finally asked Jesse if all his sons were actually here. And Jesse was forced to respond that there was one son, the youngest, who was out keeping the sheep. When Jesse sent for David and Samuel finally saw him, the Lord to said to Samuel, *"Arise, anoint him, for this is he"* (1 Samuel 16:12). And David was anointed king by Samuel in front of his brothers.

No one even thought to invite young David to Samuel's ceremony. Besides, someone had to watch over the sheep. But little did anyone know that as he shepherded his little flock in the wilderness, God was watching, training, and cultivating David's heart for Himself, even teaching him that he could do extraordinary things with the strength of the Lord.

Can you imagine David moseying around the field, composing a song of praise for God, when all of a sudden he sees a lion approach, ready to take out one of his favorite young lambs? Suddenly, he can feel the power of the Lord come upon him with strength and give him skills that are beyond him. He swiftly takes out the lion before it can harm any of his sheep, shocked and amazed at what just happened. I can imagine him thinking like young boys do: *Did anyone see that? That was amazing. No one's going to believe me if I tell them what just happened.* And then to his delight, the same thing happens a few weeks later with a bear. David becomes so used to this happening that he knows beyond a doubt that God is with him, granting him the skills and power to protect the sheep. And all the while God is preparing him in the secret place, building his faith in the strength of the Lord and building in David a deep confidence in God. This is what young David says to King Saul when he is told he is too young and not allowed to go out and fight Goliath:

> *"'Your servant has struck down both lions and bears, and this uncircumcised Philistine shall be like one of them, for he has defied the armies of the living God.' And David said, 'The Lord who delivered me from the paw of the lion and from the paw of the bear will deliver me from the hand of this Philistine.' And Saul said to David, 'Go, and the Lord be with you!'"* (1 Samuel 17:36-37)

Once again David is thought to be too young to go out to battle and tries to convince the king that he is able to fight the giant despite his lack of military experience. But just as God chose unlikely David from among all his brothers, this young man is chosen once again by God to lead the armies of Israel to victory by taking down the arrogant giant. The Lord was most certainly with him.

I never would have opened my mouth to be the speaker for the ladies retreat if I hadn't first experienced what it was like to be flooded with God thoughts in private. In the days leading up to the retreat, the message God was giving me became more powerful and more important than my fears. Even though I had never spoken at an event like this before, I had confidence in God that was forged in the secret place, by abiding in Christ. The Lord is in the habit of choosing the most unlikely leaders, training them in secret, and at just the right time bringing them out of hiding to do what He alone can do through them. Has God been training you for something? I'm sure David didn't imagine that the lowly work of shepherding was preparing him to be a warrior and future king, but God is able to use our everyday circumstances to prepare us. And while the preparation is happening, we don't always know why.

We don't always know that the simple mundane moments of our lives might be the very thing that God is using to prepare us for His assignment. You may not know until that moment, when the promptings of the Holy Spirit are telling us to speak up or do something. David knew it when he saw the giant Goliath taunting his people and cursing the name of his God. He instinctively knew that the strength of this large man was still no match for the strength of his God. David knew it was time to once again go after "the lion and the bear" in order to protect the sheep and to show off Who God is and what He is capable of to the Philistines and Israelites alike. How is God preparing you? And maybe more importantly, what is He preparing you for? In the world's eyes, you might be the most unlikely leader for the job. But what is Jesus telling you?

Jesus, the True and Better David
Born in obscurity with rumors of scandal, Jesus was an unlikely leader in the minds of the religious leaders of the day. They were looking for a Messiah with power, position, and means and Jesus wasn't what they had in mind. And yet, He was exactly Who we needed. A High Priest Who is able to identify with us in every way and never give in to temptation. He is the Mediator, working on our behalf, Who knows what it's like to be us, and at the same time, knows what it's like to be God.

Just as David was tested with an attack from a lion and a bear in those isolated sheep fields, Jesus too was led away to a desolate place to be tested: *"Then Jesus was led up by the Spirit into the wilderness to be tempted by the devil"* (Matthew 4:1). For 40 days and nights, Jesus had nothing but the presence and direction of His Father. He spent large amounts of time with God, listening for Him, and being trained by the Holy Spirit. When the devil came with temptation and vicious attacks, Jesus faced Satan with the weapon He was most skilled in—the weapon of Scripture. David faced his enemy with a sling, but the true and better David faced His enemy with the authority and power of the Word of God.

Jesus is reflected in the life of David because He is the One, not you or me, who takes down our enemy and rescues us from his grip and oppression. Just as David wasn't the true hero that day —it was the Spirit of God, coming upon him to accomplish what no seasoned warrior in the Israelite army was willing or able to do—so God chose an unlikely boy with a slingshot and a few stones to showcase His power. With one strong blow to the head, David took down the giant and cut off his head once and for all so that the men of Israel could go forth to fight in victory. It all points to Jesus Who took down the devil and his entire kingdom with one act of courage and sacrifice. Hebrews tells us that,

> *"When Christ had offered for all time a single sacrifice for sins, he sat down at the right hand of God, waiting from that time until his enemies should be made a footstool for his feet. For by a single offering he has perfected for all time those who are being sanctified."* (Hebrews 10:14)

Jesus won the ultimate victory against sin and death.

Because of Jesus, we too go forth and fight our battles in victory. We are trained in the secret place, sometimes even in the wilderness to receive our instructions. It is there that we know Who really does the work and how we get to be a part of it.

Unlikely leaders are all over the world, representing Him to those who have yet to see His power on display. Are you next?

Craig's Response

I love the phrase "forged in the secret place." This is where God shapes unlikely leaders for His glory. David was the youngest of the siblings, taunted by his brothers, and the most unlikely of all choices. Yet God told Samuel that He does not look at outward appearance, He looks at the heart. When God looked at David, He saw a young man who had a heart that pursued God. His leadership strength was forged in the secret place.

So much of what we do as leaders is done in public on center stage. But if the platform of leadership is not supported by the privacy of abiding with Jesus back stage, then our leadership will implode. Skills alone do not make one a leader. Natural giftedness does not make one a leader. It is God's extraordinary power working through the lives of ordinary people that turns unlikely people into leaders for His glory. David did not fit in Saul's armor. Nor do we fit in anyone else's shoes. As leaders, we must have a unique walk with God where He prepares us for the path of leadership He calls us to.

Chapter Five
The Unwilling Leader: Jonah
Craig Trierweiler

"But Jonah rose to flee to Tarshish from the
presence of the Lord..."
Jonah 1:3

Bend the Knee

In 2016, Kori and I had the privilege of joining a biblical study
tour in Israel. As we traveled through the Holy Land, our group
gathered around our teacher, Eric Schrotenboer, as he connected
the dots of biblical history. One of the great lessons Eric taught
about the life of Jesus was the importance of living in a posture
of submission and humility, something he called "bending the
knee." As we considered the life of Jesus, it was clear that He not
only modeled "bending the knee," but also commanded that
those who follow Him do the same. In other words, God is
looking for people who are willing to obey Him in a life of
humble service. But what about leaders who are unwilling?
What happens to those who refuse to yield to the command of
God? God knows that the best way to get us to bend the knee, is
by using pain and difficulties to draw us closer to Himself and
realign our priorities with His.

During the hardest stretch of my ministry career, God took me
through a school of brokenness in order to teach me to bend the
knee. During that season, I sat at a local restaurant with a

mentor sharing the struggles I was facing. He leaned over the table, lowered his glasses, and lovingly identified that the core issue was my need to honor God by honoring the authorities over me. He reassured me with a thought from an old saint: *"God will not use greatly whom He has not hurt deeply."* [4]

What he meant is that God often leads His people through a season of brokenness, chisels away at rough edges of stubborn pride, and then is able to use them in far greater ways for His glory. In other words, with the calling that God had placed on my life, I had a choice of being willing or unwilling to bend the knee. My choice would come with big consequences. Consider the words of Isaiah: *"If you are willing and obedient, you shall eat the good of the land; but if you refuse and rebel, you shall be eaten by the sword"* (1:19-20).

Throughout Scripture, we see that those who are willing to obey the Lord open themselves to be used in great ways, whereas those who are unwilling to bend the knee limit the work God can do through them and often experience painful consequences. Pastor Scotty Smith writes, *"Until leaders have suffered, and have learned to steward their pain, they don't really have much to offer."* [5] Before the season of brokenness in my life, I had a bachelor's degree in Pastoral Studies and positional authority in the local church, but I had little to offer because I had not yet learned the posture of bending the knee. God was using the school of brokenness to produce in me a doctoral degree in humility.

Jonah, the Unwilling Leader
There is no greater leadership paradox in the Bible than Jonah. He is a perfect case study of an unwilling leader whom God had to take through a painful season of brokenness in order to give him a willing and obedient heart. His story shows how relentless God is in pursuing reluctant leaders. He is willing to go to great lengths to accomplish His purposes.

Jonah was a prophet, pastor, and teacher. Whatever title you give him, Jonah was called to deliver God's word to the residents of Nineveh, the chief adversaries of Israel. The thought of proclaiming a message of repentance to Israel's enemies was something Jonah simply was unwilling to do. Jonah was given a message from heaven to a people who he thought deserved hell. God called Jonah to obey, but Jonah was completely unwilling to bend the knee. Everything in his posture stood in rebellion to God's call.

His story begins by refusing God's command and then moving in the complete opposite direction. Have you ever done that? When God told the prophet to go to Nineveh, Scripture says *"Jonah fled."* In other words, when God called Jonah to go east, Jonah went west. When God told him to travel by land, Jonah boarded a ship, and traveled by sea instead. No doubt there are people like this in every church in America. God gives a clear call to obey or submit, and they go in the opposite direction. They refuse God's word and are unwilling to bend the knee. Acting like Jonah, they board a ship of rebellion and try to do life outside the authority of God. When we do that, we put ourselves in a position where we experience the loving, but firm discipline of the Lord.

When Jonah tried to run, God pursued him with a storm. When Jonah was thrown overboard by his shipmates, God sent a fish to swallow him. Jonah's unwillingness put him in deep water of painful consequences. Sometimes it takes a three-night stay in an underwater sleazy motel to get people to bend the knee and be willing to submit to God's call. Moments like this are described as life-altering, bottom-of-the-barrel, broken-and-submitted wake-up calls.

In chapter 2, Jonah finally waves a white flag of surrender and bends the knee to the Lord. Kneeling inside the stomach of a fish, Jonah submits: *"But I with the voice of thanksgiving will sacrifice to you; what I have vowed I will pay. Salvation belongs to the Lord!"* (Jonah 2:9). In other words, *"Okay, God, you got my attention. This fish stinks. I'll do what you want!"* This was Jonah's graduation ceremony from the school of brokenness. God had chased him down and Jonah finally bent the knee with a willing and obedient spirit. When God commanded the fish to spit Jonah on dry land, Jonah was finally headed in the right direction with the right message. God had relentlessly pursued Jonah and overcame his reluctant spirit.

This is a common pattern for how God pursues reluctant, unwilling leaders and leads them through a school of brokenness. He calls us to obey, gives us the freedom to choose, and then lovingly allows us to taste the consequences of our disobedience. But in spite of our unwillingness, He chases us down until we finally bend the knee in surrender. The moment we wave the white flag of surrender is our final exam in God's doctoral program. At that moment, God hands us a diploma and we are finally ready to be used by God in greater ways. That is Jonah's story. That is our story.

Initially, when God told Jonah to preach a message of repentance, Jonah refused because he wanted the people of Nineveh to be punished. But once he bent his knee and was willing to obey the Lord, Jonah became the great evangelist of Nineveh. Thousands were converted under his evangelistic crusade. The city was spared disaster. Jonah should have rejoiced, gone on a speaking tour, and written a book called *God's Relentless Pursuit of Reluctant Leaders.* Instead, Jonah raged against God because he did not want God to show mercy. His response shows just how deeply ingrained was his prejudice against the people of Nineveh:

"But it displeased Jonah exceedingly, and he was angry. And he prayed to the Lord and said, 'O Lord, is not this what I said when I was yet in my country? That is why I made haste to flee to Tarshish; for I knew that you are a gracious God and merciful, slow to anger and abounding in steadfast love, and relenting from disaster. Therefore now, O Lord, please take my life from me, for it is better for me to die than to live.'" (Jonah 4:1-3)

What a paradox of a preacher! When the people of Nineveh called on the Lord to receive forgiveness, Jonah pouted because God showed mercy instead of judgment.

Could you imagine any missionary sending such a report back home to their supporters? *"Fellow supporters, this last month has been aggravating. We have seen God extend mercy to sinners, heal the lame, and perform miracles. Entire villages have been converted to Christ. We are discouraged by this because these people deserve judgment and we have been praying for their disaster. Our anger toward God is so deep that we would rather die than witness any further nonsense. In light of these recent tragedies, we have no other choice than to return from the mission field."*

Crazy, right? And yet, in the midst of being used by God, Jonah still shows characteristics of an unwilling leader who is not fully surrendered. To say it another way, Jonah began without bending a knee. In the fish, he bent one knee in submission to God. But it appears that Jonah refused to bend both knees in full surrender to the Lord. Where have you been partially willing to obey God?

God's School of Brokenness
During my season of brokenness, I had to learn the posture of full and complete surrender to the will of God. During that time, I read a book called *A Tale of Three Kings* by Gene Edwards.[6] It is written in story form about the lives of three Old Testament kings: Saul, David, and Absalom and how each of them responded to authority. As the story unfolds, it is clear that Saul and Absalom had rebellious hearts that refused to bend the knee to God's authority. As I wept my way through the pages, I realized how often my heart was like theirs. I too am prone to an unwilling heart that rejects God's call, justifies wrongdoing, and stands in total defiance to God. My heart marveled at David's willingness to bend the knee, honor authority, and humble himself under the hand of God.

Just like the turning point in Jonah's life was when he surrendered to God, my transformation took place when I finally learned to kneel in surrender to God's will. God had chased me down, allowed me to experience the deep waters of pain, put me through a school of brokenness, and reshaped my heart to make me usable for the work of ministry. This is what God does: He relentlessly pursues reluctant leaders until we willingly bend the knee in submission to Him.

Three Postures to the Call of God

The way I see it, the life of Jonah presents three different ways people respond to God when He calls us to obey. I call it No-Knee (stubbornly unwilling), One-Knee (partially willing), and Two-Knee (totally willing):

- **No Knee:** Jonah's story began with an unwillingness to bend his knees in submission to God. God called him to a task, and Jonah refused to go. His unwillingness to bend his knees is a warning to all of us about the consequences that await those who refuse God's calling. If we are unwilling to obey God, we too may find ourselves in deep water. When God calls us, He is asking us to bend the knee and be willing to obey Him. Sometimes the cost is high. Sometimes God may even call us in a direction we don't want to go. But refusing to bend our knees will ultimately lead to a season of brokenness as God relentlessly pursues us to submit to His will.

- **One Knee:** As Jonah's story unfolds, he seems to bend a knee and be willing to obey God. He waved a white flag of surrender. But over time, his attitude revealed that one knee was still raised in rebellion to God's call. His attitude at the end of the book shows how deeply reluctant he was to obey God. Like a rebellious peasant who is forced to kneel before a king, Jonah was kneeling on the outside, but standing up on the inside. The good news is that God still used this reluctant leader to

42

accomplish His will. There are many people like Jonah who do things half-heartedly or reluctantly. They are "one-knee" leaders who are willing to obey but with reluctance. One of the great transitions we need to make as leaders, as Mike Berkley says, is *"to move from reluctant leader to eager leader."*[7] The book of Jonah ends abruptly, with the prophet whining about God's grace, showing he never made the transition to an eager leader. Perhaps there is an area where you are only bending one knee to God. Perhaps you lack eagerness to serve God with joy. If so, learn from the prophet Jonah as God calls you to a life of eager service. Even the apostle Peter, who himself had to learn through seasons of brokenness, taught leaders of the church to shepherd the flock of God *"willingly and eagerly"* (see 1 Peter 5:1-4).

- **Two Knees:** I'm not sure Jonah ever surrendered with total willingness to God's call. After his brokenness, Jonah was willing to obey, but the way he responds at the end shows that both knees were not bent in surrender to God. What about you? Are you the type of leader who willingly bends both knees in submission to God? When God calls you east, do you go east willingly? When God calls you to preach, do you preach willingly? When God calls you to obey, do you obey with a willing and obedient heart? When God does His work through you, do you rejoice that He chose to use you, an *unqualified, unprepared, unsatisfied, unworthy, unfit, unwilling, undeserving* leader?

Yet, here is the mystery in it all. God relentlessly pursued this reluctant leader and literally brought him to his knees in order to use Jonah for His glory. It reminds me of the great writer C.S. Lewis who described himself as "the most dejected and reluctant convert in all England." In a 2016 *Chicago Tribune* article about C.S. Lewis, the author writes, "And it's that reluctance along with the astonishing lucidity of his prose, the open-hearted spirit of his storytelling and the exquisite rigor behind his intellect, that have combined to make C.S. Lewis pretty much every atheist's favorite Christian thinker."[8] It is amazing that God pursues reluctant, unwilling people, trains them in a school of brokenness, and then uses them to accomplish his work!

Jesus, the True and Better Jonah

It is no wonder that Jesus is a perfect contrast to this reluctant prophet who was unwilling to obey God's call. Jesus willingly entered into the world, taught His disciples to bend the knee, and proclaimed the same message as Jonah: *"Repent, for the Kingdom of Heaven is near."* Whereas Jonah was unwilling to surrender, Jesus went into Gethsemane and fell on His knees in total submission: *"Father, if you are willing, remove this cup from me. Nevertheless, not my will, but yours, be done"* (Luke 22:42). That is total, unconditional surrender to the Father.

That is the prayer of a willing leader. This was Jesus' final moment of surrender where He was fully willing to submit to the Father's will and embrace the cross. Jesus did this to open Heaven for a people who deserved Hell. And just as Jonah spent 3 days in an underwater prison, so Jesus was locked away in a tomb for 3 days until He burst forth in glorious resurrection power. In an ironic weaving of their two stories, Jonah's prayer of reluctance from the belly of the fish later becomes the victorious triumph of the risen church: *"Salvation belongs to the Lord!"* (Revelation 7:10). May the members of Jesus' church learn the posture of bending our knees in total and irrevocable surrender to our King.

Kori's Response

It was our first fight as a married couple. We were choosing our first apartment together and Craig and I did NOT see eye to eye. He wanted a smaller apartment with the better location. I wanted a nicer apartment that was further away. It was gridlock until Craig sat me down and gently told me, "Kori, I know you want your pick on the apartment and I would love to give it to you, but I have to make what I think is the best decision for us. We need to go with the smaller apartment." He made the final call and it was not what I wanted. But I did have a choice about how I would respond. I could make him pay with silent protest, a bad attitude, or bitter remarks throughout the two-year stay in that apartment. Or I could "bend the knee" and trust God with Craig's decision. Within weeks upon settling into our first home, we both knew that it was the best decision. I look back on that apartment with such great fondness now. I bent the knee and was able to see God's abundant blessing and favor being poured out.

Chapter Six
The Untrained Leader: Gideon
Kori Trierweiler

"Where are all his wonders that our ancestors told us about when they said, 'Did not the Lord bring us up out of Egypt?' But now the Lord has abandoned us and given us into the hand of Midian."
Judges 6:13

I am the most insecure person I know. I even feel a bit nervous admitting that to you. Maybe it's because I know myself better than I know anyone else, but that's how I feel. Seriously, it seems like I can't handle any criticism without being bombarded with insecurities and self-doubt. Growing up, I always felt inferior to others. From my view, everyone else seemed far smarter, more competent, better looking, and easily confident. I assumed everyone around me was in the "know" and I was the only one faking it, trying desperately not to be found out. I know those thoughts aren't true, but they have been my companions for years. My natural response to these fears has been to hide.

I don't like sitting in the front row. I avoid walking in front of a room full of people. I can't stand being the center of attention, and I dreaded walking down the aisle on my wedding day because, naturally, everyone was staring at me. I like being in the background, blending in, being a nobody. I like to be, you know, one of the followers (hey, the world needs followers too).

But if I'm honest, this is the way I like it because being a follower is safer. If you're not seen, then there is less chance you will be embarrassed, criticized, rejected, critiqued, or have people disappointed in you for not meeting their expectations.

I began to see that so much of how I defined myself and my interactions with others was based on fear. I was afraid of what others thought of me, I was afraid of failing them, and I was afraid that if I didn't find out what people wanted from me and meet their expectations then they would be angry with me, reject me, and walk away once and for all.

Gideon, the Untrained Leader

All throughout Scripture it seems like God intentionally looks for the most unsuitable, unassuming, even unwilling people to accomplish His great purposes. In the book of Judges, He is doing that exact thing. Imagine with me the situation here: Your entire country is overcrowded. An arrogant multitude of people called the Midianites have been taking over your land. They have been there for seven long years and have sufficiently gobbled up what limited resources are left.

You, Gideon, are simply trying to survive by keeping your head down and trying not to draw attention to yourself. These oppressive people are like a swarm of locusts, too large for your small family to take on, and you have seen them take what they want, when they want it...or else. You are living in hopeless and desperate times. All those stories you heard growing up about a God who fought and protected His people seem like an ancient myth in light of the current trouble you're in. The only goal now is to stay alive for another season.

This is where Gideon is when the Lord Almighty comes and meets with him. He is secretly threshing wheat in a wine press to keep it from the greedy grip of the enemy, and all of a sudden he has an unexpected meeting:

> *"And the angel of the Lord appeared to Gideon, he said, 'The Lord is with you, mighty warrior.' 'Pardon me, my lord,'*

> *Gideon replied, 'but if the Lord is with us, why has all this happened to us? Where are all his wonders that our ancestors told us about when they said, "Did not the Lord bring us up out of Egypt?" But now the Lord has abandoned us and given us into the hand of Midian.'* (Judges 6:12-13)

What is this? Mighty warrior? The angel of the Lord was speaking to him? Can't you see Gideon do a quick glance behind him to double check that the message is indeed meant for him? Yep, no one else here but him. Incredible. And the Lord called him a mighty warrior? What is He talking about? Gideon knows he hasn't had any military training. He's not a warrior, let alone a mighty one! And he's got some questions for the Lord.

I love how honest Gideon is with his doubtful and somewhat accusing answer. Excuse me, God, but how can you possibly say that you are with us when our living conditions are so bleak? We are hiding in caves, hoarding food, and barely surviving against these wicked, brutal people. Where have you been?

But God responds to Gideon's doubts:
> *"And the Lord turned to him and said, 'Go in the strength you have and save Israel out of Midian's hand. Am I not sending you?' And he said to him, 'Please, Lord, how can I save Israel? Behold, my clan is the weakest in Manasseh, and I am the least in my father's house.'"* (Judges 6:14-15)

Gideon was being commissioned to do a job he didn't ask for and was never trained to do. And from his view this undertaking had very high stakes and almost certain failure. That's how scary, unexpected, and shocking this assignment must have seemed to Gideon. So he tries to explain the situation to the Lord. "You see God, I'm a nobody! In fact, I'm a nobody of nobodies—the weakest and the least of my clan and my family. No one is going listen to me let alone follow me into battle." Yet God replies to Gideon's fears with a simple but powerful promise: *"I will be with you, and you will strike down all the Midianites, leaving none alive"* (v. 16).

Even though Gideon had no training and probably had no idea where to begin, the message that the Lord gives Gideon is crucial. He promises Gideon three things:
1. I am with you!
2. You are a mighty warrior.
3. I will defeat the enemy.

In other words, He is saying, "Gideon, you are not alone in this fight. I will lead you and instruct you every step of the way. I am going to use you to bring about the victory. And by the way, you are a mighty warrior! This is how I see you because I know everything about you and I know the plans I have for you."

The Calling
I completely identify with Gideon. There was a particular time in my life where I remember thinking the same thing. *You want me to do what, Lord? I know You don't make mistakes but it seems like You got it wrong this time. I'm not qualified. I'm not smart enough. I don't know what I'm doing and will most certainly mess it all up. What will my family think? What if they don't believe me when I tell them what You told me to do?*

I mentally compiled a list of people I knew would be better suited for the job God had assigned to me. I tried pointing to them as suitable alternatives to this crazy plan He had. But God was relentless in His choice of me. He kept saying He wanted me for this task. He even seemed to imply that I was His first pick. I was afraid and intimidated. I was mid-panic attack and that's when I heard it. My new name. The Lord whispered a word to me that changed everything. ***"Kori, I am with you and I have made you to be Fearless."***

God and I both know how deeply vulnerable and insecure I am. He also knew I had not one ounce of training for what He was calling me to...but He called me anyway. From fearful to fearless.

He hid me away in His presence, in the secret place, and trained me by filling me with His confidence, power, and strength. He patiently trained my hands for battle, telling me what to do and how to do it. He stooped down to where I was and lifted me up to make me great.

I have discovered that God loves my weaknesses. My inability, doubts, fears, and insecurities are a perfect match for His confidence, power, and strength. He didn't choose me for the job in spite of my weaknesses, but because of them. My weaknesses are the best place to showcase His glory! His power truly is made perfect in weakness. From God's view, I'm a perfect candidate for the job. There is nothing like being met by your Creator with His promise to help and His glimpse of how He sees you. So often it is the very opposite of the message the world has sent us all throughout our years.

Even though Gideon encountered God and was given the name of Mighty Warrior, he still had his doubts. Was this really God talking to him? Would God really do this amazing thing through him? And so Gideon came up with a plan to make sure God really was calling this untrained leader to lead. He would lay out a fleece of wool on the ground at night, and he asked that if *"there is dew on the fleece alone, and it is dry on all the ground, then I shall know that you will save Israel by my hand, as you have said."* And Gideon got his answer. In the morning the fleece was wet and the ground was bone dry. But it wasn't quite enough for Gideon. So he asked the Lord again. Can you do the same thing, but basically reverse it? If I leave the fleece out on the ground, *"Please let it be dry on the fleece only, and on all the ground let there be dew."* And we are told God did just as Gideon asked (Judges 6:36-40).

Was this really God talking to him? He asked God to confirm it, and miraculously, God did. Then he said, "That's great God, but just in case it was a fluke, could You confirm it again?" And miraculously, God did it again. I know that Gideon sometimes gets a bad rap for asking God to prove Himself again and again, but I want to focus less on Gideon and more on how God responds to Gideon's doubts.

Have you ever been there? I have. It's a place where you think God is talking to you, but you have some questions. And before you step out to do it, you just NEED to make sure it's really Him and not just your own imagination. I take great comfort in how God responded to timid, untrained, uncertain Gideon. With all his "fleecing" Gideon is asking, "God, would you please reassure me and confirm to me that I can really trust You?" God isn't angry with Gideon's doubts; He walks with him through all his double-checking and clarifying questions. God answered him, patiently repeated Himself, and reassured Gideon.

This was on-the-spot faith training—an acceleration of spiritual growth. Remember, Gideon had never before encountered God personally, and this was his crash-course training that God could do the impossible and could be trusted. Gideon didn't need a bunch of military training to be a mighty warrior. He just needed faith training. And God graciously met his every fear, doubt, and insecurity. Gideon looked and probably felt nothing like a mighty warrior that day, but the God who sees everything —past, present, and future—knew and called him out to be the man he truly was. He called him a mighty warrior as if he already was one. From God's perspective, it was already a done deal, already happened, past-tense.

The Naming of a Child
When England's Duke and Duchess of Cambridge, William and Catherine's first child was born, he was given a very big name with honor, title, and position. It was announced to England and all the world that on July 22, 2013, "His Royal Highness Prince George of Cambridge" had been born. This baby was no ordinary boy. Before he could even walk, talk, or have a clue who he really was, he was declared to be His Royal Highness Prince George of Cambridge. Such a big name for a mere infant. No doubt as he grows he will come to understand who he belongs to and who he really is: royal, important, famous,

wanted, and celebrated by the entire country. He will have to grow into that name and all that the title and position holds for him. In some ways, he will have to be taught, trained, and shown how to become who he already is.

This is similar to our new birth into the Kingdom of Heaven. Because of sin and the negative messages of this world, we don't always see ourselves clearly. We need to be trained to become the person God already knows us to be. We need to allow Him to give us a new name. Sometimes when I look at the world around me and the environment I live in, I forget my new name, and He has to remind me often. When I am afraid, and tell God I don't know how to do this, I hear: *Be Fearless, My child.* He assures me that I already am because that is who He made me to be. I'm still learning how to live up to my name, but I am not alone in the training.

Jesus, the True and Better Gideon
From the world's perspective, Jesus was a nobody. He wasn't born in a palace, with title, servants, and a prestigious role to inherit. Rather He was born in a manger to parents with a history of scandal and gossip that surrounded His birth. As a boy, His training was in carpentry because it was His earthy father's trade. He was raised in a small, insignificant village called Nazareth in the area of Galilee. He must have seemed like a pretty average boy to most people who knew Him and not the Ruler, Leader, Redeemer, Warrior, and Savior of all mankind— The very Son of God!

Yet God chose Jesus to be born in obscurity, raised in anonymity, and hidden away until the appointed time, all the while He was working out His plan of salvation for us. For Jesus, the seemingly "untrained" leader, would fight and defeat the entire kingdom of darkness, victoriously leading His people out of the death-grip of sin and the oppressive captivity of Satan. Jesus is the true and better Gideon because He, unlike Gideon, always knew Who He was and what He came to do for us. Jesus is the true and better Mighty Warrior who stooped down, picked out the untrained Gideon and transformed him by giving him a high calling and new name to match it. And Christ longs to do this with you as well.

Our Father God is all about naming His children with title, position, and honor. With our new kingdom, we too receive a new name, and a new calling. And it is all because there is one name that is truer and better than all the rest. It is the highly exalted, all-powerful, all-authoritative name of JESUS:

> *"Therefore God has highly exalted him and bestowed on him the name that is above every name, so that at the name of Jesus every knee should bow, in heaven and on earth and under the earth, and every tongue confess that Jesus Christ is Lord, to the glory of God the Father."* (Philippians 2:9-11)

We need to become who we already are in the sight of the Lord. We do that by spending time with Him, listening for our new name, and growing up spiritually into that name by the power of *His* name—Jesus.

Craig's Response
"The Lord is with you, mighty warrior." Gideon must have chuckled because he was anything but mighty or a warrior. I love that God speaks future into Gideon. He speaks what he will become! For my entire life, I have carried an old name around with me. The old name is: TOLERATED. Deep in my heart, I am with Gideon in the wine press, hiding in fear from other people's opinions because I feel unacceptable and merely tolerated.

But over the years, the Lord has given me a new name which is almost hard to accept. I don't always believe it. I don't always live up to it. But God has renamed me: TREASURED. Who is this God, who can take a man who feels like a tolerated nuisance and call him a treasured son? Gideon's story was from wimp to warrior. Kori's story was from fearful to fearless. My story is tolerated to treasured. What's your story?

Chapter Seven
The Unforeseen Leader: Abigail
Kori Trierweiler

"She fell at his feet and said, 'On me alone, my lord,
be the guilt. Please let your servant
speak in your ears...'"
1 Samuel 25:24

Sometimes we think leadership looks a certain way, but leadership roles can come in all different shapes and sizes. When you think of leadership, you may picture a position up front with a large following. Leadership in God's economy may look totally different than what the world praises as a successful leader. God places high importance on the unseen leader who is willing to serve Him without an audience or the praises of the masses. God values ordinary people who are willing leave their comfort zone in order to go after that one lost sheep. God honors those who allow God to interrupt their day, take the lead if necessary, and obey Him immediately.

I was out on a run. It was a beautiful morning and I was cruising along one of my favorite trails. No one was around, just me, Jesus, and the sunshine. I was tracking my pace and was pretty impressed with my timing when I first heard the noise. It sounded like someone was crying. Actually, the sound was sobbing. And the voice of the young lad sounded frightened and vulnerable. Something was wrong and I could feel it. As I rounded the bend, I finally saw him and my heart gasped. It was a three-year-old, blond-headed boy out in the middle of nowhere with tears streaming down his face. It was a heart-wrenching sight. He was clinging to the fence and with gulping cries that were barely recognizable, he wailed, "I...want...my...mommy!"

I could tell he had been wandering and crying for quite some time and finally settled there in a heap. His face was dirty from tear stains, his nose was running, and his strength was all but gone by the time I came along. From the moment I saw him, my record breaking run was totally forgotten. My mother's heart broke to see this lost boy, so vulnerable, helpless, and unprotected with no one watching over him. It was time for me to take action. There was no one else around and he needed me.

I approached him and felt that somehow he instinctively knew that I too was a mommy, somebody he could trust. "Hi, buddy, what's your name?" It took me three times before I could hear him correctly. "Owen," he said, scared and defeated. A fierce fight rose up in me for this boy and I was not going to leave him until he was safe. "Hi, Owen, I'm not going to leave you until we find your mommy. I know she is looking for you. Can you tell me what your mommy's name is?" He stopped crying long enough to look at me and with confusion he answered confidently, "Mommy!" That wasn't a lot of information to go on. All I could do was gently pat him on the back and pray, *Oh Lord, help me find this boy's mom.*

Abigail, the Unforeseen Leader
I love the story of Abigail. She is a wise, beautiful, and influential woman who is a capable and righteous manager of her home. One day, she found herself in a situation where she HAD to take immediate action for the sake of her husband and household. The Bible says that Abigail was married to a foolish, selfish, and indulgent man named Nabal.

Nabal was a man who made a lot of bad decisions in life, but this one was a deadly mistake. He insulted David, the future king of the land and refused gifts of honor to his men. David and his men dwelt in the land of Nabal and while they were there, they protected him and his estate from harm. It was customary at harvest time for those in the land who benefited from the military to give gifts of provisions for the troops. But when the harvest came, instead of the customary provision, Nabal mocked David, basically saying that David was a nobody who had gone rogue from his master.

Offended and seeking vengeance, David and his men returned to kill Nabal and his entire household when the lovely Abigail heard what her foolish husband had done. No doubt, she was used to running interference for his mistakes in the past, but this was much different. David, the man of God, was on his way to kill all of them. What could she do? Who would come to save them? She had to take the lead. There was no one else.

Quickly, she sent ahead an abundance of provisions to soften David's anger, and she prepared herself to meet him on the path before he reached her beloved home. She alone stood in the gap between death and life for her entire household. Abigail didn't know what would happen. She didn't know how David would respond to her or if he would even listen to her. He could have just killed her on the spot and continued on to finish the job. Her experience with her husband had taught her that men were reckless in their decisions and rash in their anger. But she had also learned how to stay calm and approach the situation with grace and wisdom. This time was no different, though much more was at stake.

In preparation to meet an angry army, she composed herself and began to formulate the words she would use to save their lives. Intent on slaughtering Nabal's clan, David came to a screeching halt when he met a lone woman on a donkey. It was Abigail, Nabal's wife. It was unexpected. This is an unforeseen turn of events for him and he was willing to listen to her. This was

Abigail's moment and she nailed it. She wove together her words beautifully to honor David, reminding him of who he was, encouraging him to disregard Nabal's comments, and keeping him from making the huge mistake of taking vengeance for himself. In one short but powerful speech, she turned his wrath into rejoicing, saving David from sin and the lives of her entire family.

The Lost Boy
He was lost and dangerously close to a busy intersection, but God knew everything and planned out Owen's protection precisely. As I stood there holding his hand for comfort and praying to the Lord about what to do next, two young ladies came running on the trail. I was able to use their cell phone to call the police. Within minutes the police officer met us at the intersection just a few yards away.

Together we pieced together the story and discovered that this boy's family was at the local campground, and early that morning he had wandered down the bike trail when I found him about a half-mile away. Thankfully, we were able to reunite him with his family.

Like Abigail, I didn't wake up that morning expecting to be thrust into a leading role in order to save lives, but that little boy needed me. He was lost, but never alone. Owen had no idea of what to do, but with God's help, I did. This event was not in my plan for the day but the God Who sees all, knows all, Who is intrinsically good and sovereign over all, saw fit to use me as the unforeseen leader/rescuer for a wayward lost child headed in the wrong direction. Just as He did all those years ago with the brave unforeseen leader, God is still using average people like us today. Would you be willing? Is God calling you to be His unforeseen leader in somebody's life today?

Jesus, the True and Better Abigail
Who would have thought in God's plan to rescue fallen mankind from the path of destruction that God would choose

the greatest, ultimate unforeseen leader of all! Our God chose His most prized possession, His greatest treasure, His one and only Son Who is His deepest love, to sacrifice unto death on our behalf in order to gain back His possession of us. What a shock that must have been for Satan to see that God would actually trade Himself for us! When we weren't even looking, this unforeseen leader took upon Himself our sin and punishment so that we could be set free to choose Him!

Abigail's life points us to Jesus who saw our arrogant ways and saved us before we even knew we needed saving. Like David's army that was coming to destroy, Jesus too intercepted the righteous wrath of God that was due us because of our sins. Like Abigail with David, Jesus met God with the provision to atone for us. His provision was His very own life. He also, like Abigail, came riding on a donkey, and He eloquently speaks a word of intercession on our behalf. Abigail told David, let the blame fall on me and me alone for the misdeeds of my husband. Jesus says that same thing for us. He saves our lives by taking the blame for us and is constantly speaking up for us, defending us, and saving us from our own folly. Abigail made peace between David and her household. Jesus makes peace between God and us. Because of Christ, God is justified and we are sanctified. Oh, What a Savior!

"Who is to condemn? Christ Jesus is the one who died—more than that, who was raised—who is at the right hand of God, who indeed is interceding for us." Romans 8:34

Craig's Response

Back when I was a kid, I would occasionally do "Nabal" things that were foolish and deserving of punishment. My dad, being the disciplinarian, would dole out punishments that were justly deserved and fairly apportioned. On one such occasion, I was the Nabal and my dad was the King David ready to discipline when "Abigail" entered the story to intervene on behalf of my crimes. My big brother, Victor, came in the room, laid on top of me, and willingly put himself between me and my dad. In other words, my elder brother loved me so much that he was willing to take the punishment I deserved upon himself! What an unforeseen and undeserved expression of love!

This is a picture of the good news of the gospel. We are all Nabals—foolish, senseless, arrogant, and deserving of judgment. But along came Jesus Christ, the true and better elder brother who willingly put Himself between us and the punishment we deserve. Abigail's story and Jesus' cross are both expressions of leaders who intervene on behalf of undeserving people.

I wonder, where are the unforeseen places where God will call us to act? Where are the unforeseen leaders that God will raise up to intercede on behalf of others? The good news of Abigail's unforeseen leadership is that we don't need a title or position to make a big impact in the life of others. We simply need a ready and willing heart as we allow God to overcome our reluctance and use us for His glory.

Chapter Eight
The Unworthy Leader: Peter
Craig Trierweiler

"Get behind me, Satan! For you are not setting your mind on the things of God, but on the things of man."
Mark 8:33

Wonder: The Movie that Made Me Weep
It was spring break 2018 and free movies were playing at the local theater. Two of my kids begged me to take them to see a movie, which I reluctantly attended thinking it was for kids. The movie was *Wonder*,[9] which follows the journey of a boy named Auggie, who was born with massive facial deformities which he tries to hide from the world. Auggie wears a space helmet so people can't see him. He feels the sting of rejection. He feels unworthy and unacceptable. He gets laughed at during the day at school only to run home to his bed where he cries, *"I am so ugly. I am so ugly."*

There I sat, on the far right side of a jammed theatre, my two kids next to me as we are eating two buckets of popcorn. Inexplicably, and almost embarrassingly, I wept as I watched the pain of Auggie come through his tears. The waterworks poured out of my eyes like an endless river. For the first 20 minutes of the movie, I thought my tears were God convicting me about how I used to bully kids who were mentally handicapped or stuttered with speech impediments. But as Auggie wept in his room, "*I am so ugly,*" it occurred to me: *I am Auggie!* His tears were hitting a core identity of my heart. My entire life I have felt ugly, unwanted, shameful, and rejected. I identify with wanting to hide behind a space helmet so that nobody sees my face. The movie kept rolling. My tears kept flowing. And my kids kept looking my way to reassure me with pats on the arm that I would be ok.

And just when I thought the tears were done, Auggie's dad (Nate Pullman), sits down with his son toward the end of the movie. Auggie was asking for his space helmet back, but his dad had hidden it and with the loving voice of a tender father, he said to Auggie: *"I know you don't always like it, but I love it. It's my son's face. I want to see it."*

More waterworks flowed down my face. The tears filling up my popcorn bucket. It was like God the Father was sitting me down, taking my face in his hands, and in the midst of my feeling unworthy, ugly, and shameful He said, *"Craig, I know you don't always like your face, but I love it. It's my son's face. I want to see it."*

During our car ride home, my kids joked and laughed about me being a cry baby. But I felt joy knowing I had just experienced the unexpected ministry of the Holy Spirit who reassured a heart that felt unworthy.

Peter, The Unworthy Man
When Jesus first called Peter to follow Him as a disciple, Peter was so moved by His power and authority he fell down at Jesus' feet and had one thing to say: *"Depart from me, for I am a sinful man, O Lord!"* (Luke 5:8).

This is Auggie in the presence of Jesus. He felt unworthy and sinful in the presence of the Almighty. Perhaps it was his past life of sin. Perhaps it was the internal ugliness of his heart. Whatever it was, Peter wanted to hide his face behind a helmet where Jesus couldn't see him for who he was. But in that tender moment, Jesus took Peter's face and said, *"Do not be afraid; from now on you will be catching men."* The Lord was in relentless pursuit of a reluctant leader and was overcoming his shame of feeling unworthy.

This is Peter's Damascus Road experience. This is his light bulb moment where Peter sees the beauty of Jesus in contrast with the ugliness of his own heart. In Chip Ingram's book *Holy Ambition,* he writes about the importance of having a high view of God and an accurate view of ourselves. Ingram writes, "Until we get a high view of God and an accurate view of ourselves, Jesus will never mean that much to us."[10] For Peter, his calling was the moment when his view of God altered his view of self and his first response was, "I'm not worthy, Lord!"

If you've ever had a moment when you were captivated by the awesome weight of God's holiness, you know how life-altering it is. Like Isaiah who saw the Lord in a glorious vision, his immediate response was, *"Woe is me! For I am lost; for I am a man of unclean lips, and I dwell in the midst of a people of unclean lips; for my eyes have seen the King, the Lord of hosts!"* (Isaiah 6:5). This is the reason Peter was a reluctant leader. Even though God relentlessly pursued him, he felt entirely unworthy because of the sinful condition of his own heart.

Throughout his years with Jesus, Peter must have wanted to hide behind a space helmet to protect his big mouth from making ridiculous comments. Both Matthew and Mark record the failed moment of this unworthy leader. Peter had just affirmed Jesus was the Christ, the Son of God. Moments later, when Jesus prophesies of His coming crucifixion, Peter takes Jesus aside to rebuke Him for such a ridiculous thought. In response, Jesus rebukes Peter and says, *"Get behind me, Satan! For you are not setting your mind on the things of God, but on the things of man"* (Mark 8:33). Imagine how unworthy you would feel if the Lord of the universe were to deliver a stinging, open rebuke! Imagine the emotional turmoil! If it were me, I'd be searching for the space helmet.

Time and time again in the Scripture, we see Peter tripping over his sandals, convincing him all the more that he is ugly and unworthy. In Galatians, his actions are so hypocritical and damaging to the church that Paul openly rebukes Peter and opposes *"him to his face, because he stood condemned"* (Galatians 2:11). And there was perhaps no worse moment than the cataclysmic failure when Peter denied three times he even knew Jesus. In case we miss how devastated Peter was, Luke records with one line how he responded: *"And he went out and wept bitterly"* (Luke 22:62).

There is Peter (Auggie) running away with a deep internal shame. He feels ugly, unworthy, and like a total failure. Imagine the overwhelming sorrow Peter must have carried. Imagine how emotionally distraught he was after having openly rejected the person he promised never to leave. He is being hounded by the scorn of the crowds and the deep shame of inner guilt. How in the world could the God of heaven ever use such an unworthy man?

One day while in Cambodia doing mission work, I went for a run on a dusty village road and was chased by a vicious group of 6 dogs who were hounding me and foaming at the mouth. After one of them bit my leg drawing blood, I found myself in a Cambodian medical clinic getting treatment. It is a terrible thing to get hounded and bit by untamed dogs.

After denying Jesus and seeing him crucified, I imagine Peter must have felt hounded by the foaming dogs of his unworthy past. As he considered his failures, hypocrisy, ignorance, and arrogance, he must have felt the poison of unworthiness sink into his skin.

But wonder of wonders, Peter found himself at a medical clinic where Jesus ministered to his wounded heart and spoke hope to this unworthy leader! When the resurrected Jesus appeared, he and Peter went for a walk on the beach. Three times Jesus asked Peter, "Do you love me?" It's almost as if Jesus was giving him three antidotes for each of his three denials. Jesus not only forgave this unworthy man, but also restored him to ministry as a key leader of the early church. How ugly Peter was on occasions! And yet how greatly the Father loved this man. It's as if the God of heaven took Peter's face in His hands and said:,*"Peter, I know you don't always like your face, but I love it. It's my son's face. I want to see it."*

God was in relentless pursuit of this reluctant leader, proving over and over that God does not call those who are worthy, but He makes worthy those He calls. Like Peter, we all may be hounded by the sinfulness of our past, but the resurrected Christ has the antidote of grace which not only forgives our inner shame, but also restores us for future ministry. What a Savior!

Battling Lies of Unworthiness
So, I rarely cry when reading books, but the tears began flowing again. I was reading *The Cry of the Soul* by Dan Allender and Tremper Longman, who began to address the internal emotions of shame and rejection. What was about to transpire totally blindsided me as it helped me identify faulty beliefs I have long held, buried beneath years of performance and position. One part in particular described me perfectly:

> "Contempt is a poison that paralyzes our deepest longing for love and meaning. It mocks our desirability. *No one wants you. No one enjoys you. You have no place with us...*Contempt isolates its victims by branding them unworthy of love. Who wants to be around a laughingstock? Mockery draws a line in the sand, separating its victim from the crowd. On the other side of the line is the in-group, laughing; near them is the silent crowd that will not risk stepping across the line to stand with the victim in his isolation. After dividing and isolating, contempt withers hope by making its victim feel foolish, deadening desire."[11]

When I read this, deep arrows of emotion penetrated my heart. I feel undesirable. I feel unworthy of love. I feel the sting of rejection. I feel like Auggie, who battles three lies that hound me every day:

1. *No one wants you.*
2. *No one enjoys you.*
3. *You have no place with us.*

Those lies have affected my friendships, family relationships, and work relations. Those lies have been reinforced during seasons of rejection, betrayal, and loss. They have caused dark seasons of depression and sorrow. They have manipulated my emotions and affected my actions. Like a deep root system, those lies have been at the core of who I am for years.

As I read further in the book, I became aware that my feelings of shame were not just about how other people viewed me. I realized that those lies were at the core of how I believed God viewed me:

1. *God does not want me.*
2. *God does not enjoy me.*
3. *God has no place for me.*

This is Auggie. This is Peter. This is me. It is the deep roots of feeling that we are undesirable and unworthy to be loved. We are unworthy to follow Jesus. And we are certainly unworthy to be leaders.

Jesus, the True and Better Peter
In the midst of our shame rises the beauty and scandal of the gospel. God took all of our shame and unworthiness and laid it upon His Son. In spite of our shame, we are not a laughingstock, but Jesus was mocked in our place. In spite of being unworthy of love, God demonstrated His love in that while we were still sinners, Christ died for us. Instead of being isolated as a victim,

we are welcomed into His Kingdom where the Father rejoices to see our face.

This is where we join Peter and every saint who has ever gone before us. God is altogether holy and we are altogether unworthy. Yet, through the death of Christ we are forgiven and restored for future ministry. Ingram continues,

> "The New Testament is filled with what? Failures! Yeah, I love that. You know why? Because I'm one. It's filled with people who failed miserably, whose lives didn't work, who were spiritually bankrupt. They came to Jesus and He cleansed and forgave them...You may think you're not qualified. Wrong! You are qualified. Christ makes you qualified to be used by God."[12]

Every single time Peter failed, he encountered the immeasurable, unending grace of the Lord Jesus. That ocean of grace is still available for every person who feels unworthy and undeserving of His love.

Christ bore our shame and guilt. In Him, our deepest longings for love and acceptance are fully met. We will never look into the eyes of God and see contempt or hatred. Because of the gospel, we can mock evil and scoff at shame. We can boast in weakness and taunt death with the confident laughter of trust. The evil one may throw shame and accusations at us, making us feel undesirable. But there stands the resurrected Christ who says:

1. *God wants you.*
2. *God enjoys you.*
3. *God has a place for you!*

I recently read a poem called "God Can Use Us All" that offers this encouragement:

"There are many reasons why God shouldn't have called you, or me, or anyone else for that matter, but God doesn't wait until we are perfect to call us...We could do wonderful things for others and still not be wonderful ourselves. Satan says, 'You're not worthy!' Jesus says, 'So what? I AM.' Satan looks back and sees our mistakes. God looks back and sees the cross."[13]

To every Auggie and Peter who feels unworthy of God's love, I say to you with full assurance: God is still in relentless pursuit of reluctant, unworthy leaders.

Kori's Response
I am not sure where it started but I remember hearing three words in my mind on replay all throughout my growing up years: **"Dumb, Stupid, Idiot."** It was like there was a recording that got played anytime I did or said something embarrassing, naïve, or foolish. It was not a nice voice and it came with such painful feelings of shame I simply wanted to hide from everything. From early on in life it became a core belief for me and I often misinterpreted looks, conversations, or situations through the belief that I was a dumb, stupid, idiot. Because I felt that way about myself, I assumed everyone else thought that about me as well.

This made for a lot of hurt feelings and false perceptions on my part. But because this belief was always there, I didn't even know it was wrong until Jesus exposed it for the thieving lie it was: *Kori, I made you and I never make stupid things.* This truth came like an "aha" moment. My life isn't about me; it is about Him. Who I am, my personality, and the way I think, all represents and points to the One Who made me. My life is worth something because of my Creator. And like the unworthy leader Peter, my value comes from the One Who sees me and absolutely loves what He has made. What a relief that God's truth sets us free.

Chapter Nine
The Unexpected Leader: Esther
Kori Trierweiler

"And who knows whether you have not come to the kingdom for such a time as this?"
Esther 4:14

I'm just a girl from Kansas. Classic small town, country cookin', wheat fields, cattle ranches, cowboy boots. You know, good, down-home people where "what you see is what you get." Growing up I felt super ordinary, a bit unimpressive, even invisible. I'm pretty sure no one looked at me growing up in that small town with my freckles and braces and said, "That girl's going to be a great leader someday!" That is, no one but Jesus. He knew all along He was going to call me to be a great leading lady, with influence, authority, purpose, and position. Don't misunderstand me, I'm not talking about greatness in the world's eyes, but rather, greatness in His!

I didn't know it at the time, but in that small town where I grew up, I was being prepared to be extraordinary. Despite how I felt, I was never invisible to God. In every circumstance, every relationship, every milkshake I made at the local Burger Shack, thinking my life was mundane and boring...God was there. I was totally unaware at the time that I was ALWAYS seen, wanted, protected, and cherished by God. And He had some pretty unexpected plans for me.

Esther, the Unexpected Leader

A young orphaned girl living in a foreign land and being raised by her uncle went through a few unexpected, even unwelcome events that brought her to her place of leadership. As a young Jewish woman just coming of age, she probably expected to marry a Jewish man of their faith and start a family. It must have been devastating for her to suddenly be rounded up by the king's soldiers, ripped from her home, and taken to the palace with a bunch of other young girls where she would never leave or see her family again. Her sole purpose was to be beautified for the pleasure of a pagan, foreign king and join the running for a slim shot at becoming his next wife. But against all odds, she was chosen to be the new Queen, and Esther found herself in a position of favor, luxury, wealth, and influence.

From the ways of this pagan kingdom, little was expected of the queen except to look beautiful and be available for the King whenever he needed her. And yet, God—Esther's God—had so much more for her to do than that. The King and leaders of the land may not have expected her to take any interest or have any influence in matters of law and decrees of the land, but in God's Kingdom she was prepared all along to be the one perfectly positioned to save His people.

Little did she know what the Lord God of Israel would require of her in her new role as Queen of Susa. Inside the safety of the palace, Esther received an urgent word from her uncle. Her people had a powerful enemy and a date was set for their complete annihilation. The Jews needed her to go to her husband, the king and plead for their lives. The problem is that no one in the land could approach the king unsummoned unless the King extended his golden scepter, thus sparing their life and allowing them access to his throne. The King hadn't asked for her for some time, and to talk to him she would have to go to him without his permission. She could wait and do nothing. Or she could go unsummoned to the King, risking her life in order to save her people. This is the advice her uncle gave her:

"For if you keep silent at this time, relief and deliverance will rise for the Jews from another place, but you and your father's house will perish. And who knows whether you have not come to the kingdom for such a time as this?" (Esther 4:14)

Esther fasted and prayed for three days and asked her people to do likewise. I bet she was hoping that God would simply prompt the King to send for her, but He didn't. When she was done praying, Queen Esther had a plan. She put on her royal robes, gathered her courage, and went unsummoned to the King, possibly walking to her death. Being disobedient to the King came with huge consequences. She had not been called for and would have been completely unexpected by him. He banished his last wife for not coming when he called; would he be furious with her now for coming when she hadn't been called? But Esther went going, not knowing what the outcome would be. For the love of her people, she had to try. And the Lord was with her and this was His plan:

"And when the king saw Queen Esther standing in the court, she won favor in his sight, and he held out to Esther the golden scepter that was in his hand. Then Esther approached and touched the tip of the scepter. And the king said to her, 'What is it, Queen Esther? What is your request? It shall be given you, even to the half of my kingdom.'" (Esther 5:2-3)

God so granted Esther favor with the king that he repeatedly asked her what she wanted, promising her that he would grant it before he even knew what the request was. With the King's good favor upon her, Esther was able to save her people. Esther's boldness and influence rescued the Jews who were once targeted and doomed for destruction. Before she stepped in, they were hopelessly marked for complete annihilation, but now because of her influence from a very powerful man, they had the upper hand. It was their enemies, not them, that were completely destroyed that day. All throughout the land the people revered, honored, and feared the Jewish people and their God. But I love this part! Even after the great victory and the King had abundantly granted her request to save her people, he couldn't help himself but ask the lovely Queen Esther again if there was anything more she wanted. With delight, he wanted to know if there was anything else he could do within his power that would make her happy.

From Ordinary to Extraordinary

From that insignificant, ordinary, small-town girl in Kansas, I have grown some in my new understanding of what Jesus has done for me. He has chosen me to belong to Him as His bride. I have been granted favor, wealth, a place of position, and authority in His Kingdom. All of this because He had me in mind as the object of His love from the very beginning. I am seated with Jesus even now at the highest spiritual position of authority, with unlimited kingdom resources at His command. But just like Esther, I have a choice of how I will respond to this amazing favor I have been given at the side of the King. I can enjoy this favor, resting in His salvation and still live for myself. Or I can engage in the work of my new kingdom that Jesus has given me.

One assignment that I know I'm called to is to be a prayer warrior—a fearless fighter of faith on behalf of my people locally and globally. I never saw myself as a prayer warrior before, but when God asked me to join Him in interceding for the lost, broken, weak, depressed, deceived, and those targeted by Satan, how could I say no? It is something He has been training me to do and the best thing about the whole process is that I get to be with Him.

In the inner chamber, the master bedchamber of the palace, if you will, I have been given favor and access to the King's heart. He has given me His love and attention and tells me to ask Him for whatever I want so that He can delightfully give it. In my spirit, I hear the Lord say to me over and over, *"Kori, what do you want? Ask me for something!"* It's as if He can't wait to hear what I will ask Him for next. He wants to know what my heart's desire is for my people. And so, alone with Him I ask Him. I ask and I ask and I keep on asking! What He does with my requests is entirely up to Him.

The kingdom work that I do is extraordinary and personal. I know beyond a shadow of a doubt that, for such a time as this, right here is my battleground. My home, my church, my city, my country, my world—these are my people to fight for in the inner chamber. I come boldly, knowing I have found favor with the King, pleading with Him to use His unlimited resources in miraculous ways on their behalf. And that means you too, my friend! I don't have to know your name to pray for you, because He does.

Jesus, the True and Better Esther

Like Esther, Jesus put Himself in harm's way in order to protect and fight for His people. But unlike Esther who was extended the scepter of life, Jesus approached God carrying the sins of the world and took the punishment that sin demands—death. He could have done nothing and safely stayed away, but instead He chose to relocate from Heaven to our world in order to become like one of us. He who never tasted the bitterness of sin, took on our sin and died on our behalf. In Him the wrath of God was poured out, the wages of sin was paid, and justice was served.

Jesus is also the true and better golden scepter of life, extended to us so that we may live and not die. All we have to do is reach out and touch it to be saved, by believing on the name of Jesus. But it gets even better! In exchange for our sin, Jesus gives us His very own royal robes of righteousness. His perfection is ours. Now we may always approach the Throne of God with freedom and confidence. Just as the Father loves, delights, and welcomes His Son Jesus into His presence, that is how much He loves, delights, and welcomes us, even beckons us to His throne of Grace.

Our roles in the kingdom of heaven are amazing and glorious, but not simply for us to sit back, relax and enjoy our secure position. We are called to something BIG! God-sized big! How could it be anything other than big when God's involved? Like Esther, for such a time as this, you are in your place of influence on purpose. We are in a war. People are dying without Jesus. God is calling unexpected leaders to bold actions, advocating for others, and to be willing to stand in the gap to reflect and represent Him.

Craig's Response

What a step of faith Esther had to take that day as she acted as an intercessor for her people! I imagine she had to overcome massive amounts of fear and reluctance in order to do what God called her to do. Her faith required courage and confidence that God would be faithful in spite of her weakness. I admire people like Esther who act with bold faith. They inspire me to be more courageous and take risks without knowing exactly how things will turn out.

I am one who needs to grow in trusting God and walking by faith in His commands. I recall one extraordinary step of faith our family took in the area of generous giving. It was such a large leap that if the parachute of God's provision didn't open, the results would be disastrous. But, our God was more than faithful to provide and prove Himself faithful.

In the leadership position God has put me in, I feel like an unexpected leader from a small town who has no ability to change circumstances or people. My big encouragement from the story of Esther is this: We can approach the hand of a loving, merciful God and ask boldly for Him to give good gifts. If Esther gained favor from a pagan king, how much more will we receive good gifts when we ask our Father in heaven? May the life of Esther remind us that God is in relentless pursuit of ordinary people who can be used to do mighty things.

Chapter Ten
The Unfit Leader: Paul
Craig Trierweiler

"I persecuted this Way to the death, binding and delivering to prison both men and women"
Acts 22:4

Unfit for Command

I am not aware of any pastor who feels fit for command. Yes, there are plenty of pastors who are arrogant or display excessive confidence. But fit? Not a chance. Not only do ministry leaders carry personal baggage and feelings of unworthiness, there are also the constant feeling that you are failing the people you are leading. I speak from the experience of an imperfect pastor who feels unfit to lead.

In his book *The Imperfect Pastor*,[14] Zach Eswine writes about the four temptations we all face as leaders. They are the temptations to:
1. Fix it all.
2. Know it all.
3. Be everywhere for all.
4. Want everything now. Immediacy

I am guilty of all four of these as a leader. I want to fix it all, know it all, be everywhere for all, and I want everything now. In other words, I want to be God. And when I realize I am incapable of doing any of those things, it makes me feel unfit to be a leader. Think of it:

- When we realize we can't **fix it all**, we feel like failures. We all face unfixable and uncontrollable situations that make us feel unfit to do our calling. We feel others would be far more suited to lead than us. Our lack of control and our inability to fix problems make us feel like we are the wrong people for the job.

- When we realize we don't **know it all**, we feel like failures. We feel like we don't have the answers to solve problems, the diplomacy to navigate challenges, or the framework to understand leadership. That lack of know-how makes us feel that we are failing the organizations we lead and also disappointing the people who follow us.

- When we realize we can't be **everywhere for all,** we feel like failures. The time demands and pressures of leadership place extraordinary demands on schedules. If we don't show up at certain events, we disappoint people who expected us to be there. If we prioritize one event over another, we are criticized for showing favoritism. And when we disappoint people and feel the sting of rejection, it makes us feel unfit to lead.

- When we realize we can't have everything **immediately,** we feel like failures. Impatience is one of the great sins of God's people and specifically of those in leadership. We want things done in our time, in our way, and without delay. And when none of that occurs, we feel unfit for leadership. As a result, Eswine says that leaders must learn how to be "long distance grace runners." [15]

The Apostle Unfit for Command

The Apostle Paul wrote a significant portion of the New Testament. He was greatly used by God, bringing salvation to Jews and Gentiles. He was a strong church planter, disciple maker, and missions motivator. He expanded the reach of the gospel throughout Turkey, Greece, and all the way to Rome.

And yet, Paul summarizes his testimony in one sentence: *"For I am the least of the apostles, unworthy to be called an apostle, because I persecuted the church of God"* (1 Corinthians 15:9).

I am the least. I am unworthy. In a human sense, Paul feels unfit for the position to which God called him. And you would feel unfit for serving the Lord if you had a testimony like Paul's. In his own words, Paul explains just how actively he opposed the message of Jesus:

> *"I persecuted this Way to the death, binding and delivering to prison both men and women"* (Acts 22:4).

> *"I myself was convinced that I ought to do many things in opposing the name of Jesus of Nazareth....I not only locked up many of the saints in prison after receiving authority from the chief priests, but when they were put to death I cast my vote against them. And I punished them often in all the synagogues and tried to make them blaspheme, and in raging fury against them I persecuted them even to foreign cities."* (Acts 26:9-11)

Many people have a checkered past, but Paul exceeds them all. He persecuted the church, bound believers in chains, and voted for the death penalty for the innocent. With all his past failures and his present weaknesses, Paul views himself as unworthy and unfit to be an apostle. And yet Paul overcame this reluctance and accepted God's call to be a leader and preacher of the gospel. This unfit leader is so compelled to preach Christ that he says, *"Necessity is laid upon me. Woe to me if I do not preach the gospel"* (1 Corinthians 9:16).

How in the world are we supposed to lead when we feel unfit for command? How can we maintain courage in leadership when we feel unable to meet the demands of those we are leading? How are leaders to remain strong when we feel the sting of rejection? What prevents us from quitting when we realize we can't fix it all, know it all, or be everywhere for all? These are the daily pressures reluctant leaders face as we not only wrestle with demands of ministry but also the emotional struggles of feeling unfit to lead.

The Daily Anxiety of Leadership

When Paul recounts all of his trials in ministry, including beatings, imprisonments, sleepless nights and shipwrecks, he ends his list of sufferings with the ultimate pressure: *"Apart from other things, there is the daily pressure on me of my anxiety for all the churches"* (2 Corinthians 11:28).

For Paul, the greatest struggle of all was not physical suffering, but the emotional turmoil of leading the church. This is the common struggle of reluctant ministry leaders: the daily pressure of anxiety for the church. And all of it makes you feel unfit to do what God has called you to do. The daily pressures feel like a crushing weight upon your chest that is immovable and uncontrollable. There are people who have needs, critics who have complaints, and ministries that have demands. In our human frailty, we simply do not have the time or energy to meet such expectations, which can produce dark seasons of hopeless anxiety.

I can't imagine Paul's pressures, but I have faced seasons in leadership where I have experienced sleepless nights, anxieties, rejections, and a combination of personal failures. I have situations I can't fix, issues I don't know how to resolve, and people I have disappointed. I can't fix it all, know it all, or be everywhere for all. At the darkest points of my journey, I couldn't sleep more than one hour a night. I was physically exhausted, emotionally drained, and spiritually empty. I would sit in a room and weep for no reason.

Doctors prescribed sleeping pills that didn't work and anti-anxiety medications that only caused me to gain weight. To counteract the anxiety, we asked our church to pray and the elders anointed me with oil. Along the way, dozens of self-appointed physicians offered their advice on the perfect cure for my troubles, none of which worked. When you are stuck in a cycle of anxiety like that, you begin to feel hopeless of things ever getting better. And when the daily pressures crush you for months, you begin to feel unfit for command and want to quit everything.

But in the face of my small trials, stands Paul who faced extraordinary pressures of church leadership. This reluctant leader feels he is the least of the apostles. The unfit leader feels unworthy to even be called an apostle. Perhaps that is why his testimony captures my heart: *"But by the grace of God I am what I am, and his grace toward me was not in vain"* (1 Corinthians 14:10).

"I am what I am." Paul does not excuse his past failures or belittle his present weakness. What he does is look with confidence to God, who relentlessly pursued him and called him into leadership. This is what makes leaders fit for command: grace! God's grace does not change our past, but it does forgive our past. God's grace does not remove our weaknesses, but it meets us in our weakness by supplying us with the strength that only God can provide. I love what Skye Jethani writes about pastors in his book *Immeasurable:* "Pastors make the worst sinners, but sinners make the best pastors."[16]

Perhaps Paul was such an excellent leader because he was such a remarkable sinner. Perhaps those of us who feel unfit for command are in the perfect place of leadership because we learn not to serve out of our own strength but by the strength of Him who supplies it (see 1 Peter 4:11). Perhaps all the anxieties of leadership help us see that *"our sufficiency is from God, who has made us competent to be ministers"* (2 Corinthians 3:5-6). In the midst of our emotional distress, there stands a God whose grace is never in vain.

Looking back on our long, arduous trek through daily pressures of leadership, there were days when we wanted to quit and walk away from it all. But God's grace sustained us, friends surrounded us, people prayed for us, and over the course of time, a light of hope began to shine through the dark clouds of despair. Because of God's goodness, the season that shook us and made everything feel unstable actually became a catalyst to realign our hearts and open doors for what God wanted to do next in our lives. I continue to marvel that God uses reluctant leaders like us for His glory and that He often does His finest work during seasons of greatest weakness.

Good News: Jesus Only Calls Unfit Leaders

So, do you feel unfit to lead? You're in good company! Do you feel that your past has disqualified you to be used by God? You are a perfect candidate! Are you reluctant to do what God has asked because you feel insignificant? Wonderful! Let me encourage you by showing that God loves to use unfit leaders for his glory:

> *"For consider your calling, brothers: **not many of you were wise** according to worldly standards, not many were powerful, **not many were of noble birth**. But **God chose what is foolish in the world to shame the wise; God chose what is weak in the world to shame the strong; God chose what is low and despised in the world**, even things that are not, to bring to nothing things that are, so that no human being might boast in the presence of God."* (1 Corinthians 1:26-29)

In other words, Jesus doesn't choose fix-it-all leaders. He chooses leaders who seem weak. Jesus doesn't choose know-it-all leaders. He chooses leaders who seem foolish. Jesus doesn't choose everywhere-for-all leaders. He chooses leaders who seem low and incapable. And the reason He does this is for one reason: That He gets the glory, not us!

Imperfect, But Perfectly Fit

So, back to Eswine's book. What do we do with those four temptations as leaders to fix it all, know it all, be everywhere for all, and want everything now? Eswine gives these action steps:

- "You were never meant to repent because you can't fix everything. You are meant to repent because you've tried."[17] In other words, God has not asked you to fix everything for everyone. For leaders like me who have tried to fix-it-all, our hope is not to control people, manipulate circumstances, or come up with solutions to every problem. Our hope is in the risen Christ, Who alone has the wisdom to meet all the demands of life and leadership. God does not call perfectly fit leaders who are capable of fixing all the problems in ministry. Rather, God calls perfectly unfit leaders who must depend on His grace to face the daily demands of ministry.

- "You were never meant to repent because you don't know it all. You are meant to repent because you've tried."[18] In other words, one of the great pressures leaders face is the expectation that we must have answers to meet the expectations of others. When people are upset, we should know what to do. When ministries are failing, we should know what the next step is. When families are falling apart, we should know the diagnosis and solution. It's called a Messiah Complex, where we assume the responsibility to know-it-all. My friend, God did not call us to know-it-all. When we admit we don't always have the answers, it helps release us from the expectations of others and look to God in greater dependency.

- "You and I were never meant to repent for not being everywhere for everybody and all at once. You and I are to repent because we've tried to be."[19] One painful reality of life and ministry is the feeling that comes when you disappoint people or fail to meet their expectations. For many leaders, we assume the guilt that we should have done more to meet their demands. I'll never forget the profanity-laced phone call of an irate church member who placed the blame of her failed marriage on me. "You should have done more. You should have helped. You should have..." It broke my heart to hear her pain. But, one of the great freedoms of

85

leadership is realizing that we cannot be everywhere for everybody all the time. As we learn to entrust people to the loving care of a sovereign God, we release the burdens of ministry to the One Person who has the ability and strength to meet people in their darkest hour.

- As for our wanting everything now, Eswine says we will have to learn that "only Jesus can fix everything, and that there are some things Jesus leaves unfixed for his glory...God will do in this awkward silence what he alone can do according to his ability" (p. 99). In other words, "a waiting of some kind will be required. Sometimes the waiting will last. No resolution will come until Jesus does."[20] For me, this is the most difficult part of leadership. When there is unresolved conflict, we feel we must do something to immediately bring resolution. When people leave the church, we feel we must do something immediately to help repair relationships. In an attempt to prove our leadership savvy, we feel that people are looking for us to immediately wave a magical wand and produce results they can see. But when things go unresolved for long periods of time, we feel the shame and guilt that we are unfit leaders who don't know what to do. But even Jesus told a parable about leaving some things unfixed until He comes again. In the parable of the wheat and weeds, the servants asked the master if they should go pull the weeds. But the master said *"No, lest in gathering the weeds you root up the wheat along with them. Let both grow together until the harvest"* (Matthew 13:29-30). My friends, one of the greatest needs of leaders is the patience required to let things remain unfixed until God works it out.

Jesus, the True and Better Paul
There is only one person Who is truly fit for command. Jesus Christ alone has the credentials and the authority to fix-it-all, know-it-all, be everywhere-for-all, and fulfill things perfectly within the framework of His divine timetable.

For leaders who feel the pressure of fixing it all, we must look to Jesus *"who works all things according to the counsel of his will"* (Ephesians 1:11). One day, we will discover that Jesus has been working behind the scenes of history to fix broken hearts and mend broken fences. When we feel unfit for leadership, we must remember that He alone has the perfect fix for man's deepest needs.

For leaders who are burdened by the need to know-it-all, we must look to Jesus, Who alone has the ability to know the hearts of all men. Jesus invites those with heavy burdens to cast their anxieties upon Him: *"Come to me, all who labor and are heavy laden, and I will give you rest. Take my yoke upon you, and learn from me, for I am gentle and lowly in heart, and you will find rest for your souls"* (Matthew 11:28-29). This is a great invitation for every leader who is weighed down by endless demands and expectations.

For leaders who find it impossible to be everywhere-for-all, we must look to Jesus, Who alone has the strength to meet the demands of what Paul called *"the daily pressure on me of my anxiety for all the churches"* (2 Corinthians 11:28). The great news for anyone who feels unfit for leadership is that the Lord Jesus has promised to build His church. No matter how much we love our church, we must remember that Jesus loves our church way more than we do. Not only that, but Jesus also has the divine ability to carry the daily pressures of His church without our help.

The Lord Jesus, in His divine wisdom, has chosen weak, unfit leaders to confound the wise. He chose Paul who considered himself the least of the apostles and used him mightily. And it's all because of God's grace. That same grace is available to us, so that we too can say: *"I am what I am and His grace is not in vain."*

Let me end with great news for all of us who feel like unfit leaders. We serve a big God who knows-it-all, fixes-it-all, is everywhere-for-all, and who does things perfectly in His timing!

What a comfort to rest in. We are unfit leaders who serve an extremely fit Savior.

Kori's Response

I love meeting with different ladies in our church. I love hearing their stories over a cup of coffee. Throughout the years, I have heard amazing stories of struggle, pain, healing, and hope. Women are awesome. There are times when I meet with women who find themselves in the midst of darkness, pain, doubt, or depression. I feel so unfit sitting across from a hurting woman who is going through something I've never been through before. She could be angry, bitter, doubting, and wanting answers to all her questions. I feel totally ill-equipped to even speak with her let alone answer her questions. That is when I take great comfort in John the Baptist's admission, *"He confessed, and did not deny, but confessed, 'I am not the Christ'"* (John 1:20).

What a great reminder, as well as a relief, that I am NOT the Savior. I don't have to fix anyone or have all the answers. I can simply listen, pray, and trust that God can handle all the issues. I don't have to "own" the situation. I don't have to smooth everything over, defend God, explain away their pain, or fix their sin issues. I am responsible for anything God calls me to do, but beyond that—"I am NOT the Christ!" He is the One responsible for their spiritual growth. When I don't know what to do or say to someone, I listen to their story and mentally place them in the lap of the loving, gracious, wise Savior. I'm so glad He knows what to do for them and how He will accomplish it. I am not the Savior. But I know who is!

Chapter Eleven
The Unclean Leader: Isaiah
Kori Trierweiler

"'Woe to me!' I cried. 'I am ruined! For I am a man of unclean lips, and I live among a people of unclean lips, and my eyes have seen the King, the Lord Almighty.'"
Isaiah 6:1-5

Apart from salvation, one of the best things Jesus has ever done for me was to show me my sin. It was a time in my life that God chose to take me through a very uncomfortable season of deep repentance. Looking back it was one of the most gracious gifts of His kindness.

You see, I was always a good girl. I grew up in a Christian home, got saved when I was five, was taught the ways of the Bible and good, clean Christianity. I didn't drink, smoke, or sleep around. I didn't get into trouble, was for the most part obedient to my parents, followed the rules—you know, the picture of the nice godly girl. But what I didn't see, the Lord could always see. And knowing what I know now, I marvel that He loved me anyway. We all sin. Some people's sins are glaringly obvious and others are more hidden. There's external sin and internal sin and Jesus had to die for it all. The thing about internal hidden sins of the heart is that sometimes they can be hidden even from us. That is, until we see ourselves in light of His pure holiness.

I followed the rules and I was good at it, so I thought. But being a good rule follower can sometimes make you look at others who aren't doing so well with a critical eye. Thoughts like, *It's not that hard, people. Just do what I do. What in the world is their problem? If they would only____then they could____.* All these can sneak into your mindset unaware. I was constantly examining myself in light of other people to see how I measured up. I felt threatened by those whose lives I thought looked better than mine, and justified by those who looked worse than mine. This attitude doesn't make for very loving, close relationships, or very good leadership skills. The sin of pride, selfishness, judgment, and self-righteousness ran rampant in my heart, but because I was so focused elsewhere, I was completely unaware of my sinful thoughts. That is, until God opened my eyes to SEE what I desperately needed to see.

Isaiah, the Unclean Leader
We meet Isaiah at a time when the nation of Judea had turned away from God, and it was time for Him to send a message to His sinful people who seemed to have forgotten all about Him. Their rebellion had gone on far too long, and God decided to raise up a leader who would fear Him, confront sin, and courageously speak His words to a nation who didn't want to hear it. But first, this leader had to have a proper view of God and a true understanding of his sin and the sins of his people. His calling came in this encounter with God:

> *"In the year that King Uzziah died, I saw the Lord, high and exalted, seated on a throne; and the train of his robe filled the temple. Above him were seraphim, each with six wings: With two wings they covered their faces, with two they covered their feet, and with two they were flying. And they were calling to one another: 'Holy, holy, holy is the Lord Almighty; the whole earth is full of his glory.' At the sound of their voices the doorposts and thresholds shook and the temple was filled with smoke.*

'Woe to me!' I cried. 'I am ruined! For I am a man of unclean lips, and I live among a people of unclean lips, and my eyes have seen the King, the Lord Almighty.'" (Isaiah 6:1-5)

Isaiah saw God in His high position on His throne and he is completely exposed. Is it not amazing that the first thing Isaiah realizes when he comes face to face with a holy God is his own sinfulness and the wickedness of his own people? And this is what has to take place for repentance to happen. What an experience! To see God and be totally laid flat by the righteousness, holiness, and perfection of Who He is, and to personally be given a glimpse of the depth of your wickedness in contrast to His flawless glory. Woe is right. And all of this was a gift leading to repentance.

Isaiah was a man who knew what it was like to truly see his sin in the light of a holy and perfect God. And for Isaiah to be the prophet and leader that God needed in that day to accomplish His will and call His people to repentance, this understanding of God's holiness in comparison to Isaiah's sin was so very necessary. A healthy fear of God can take care of so many of our issues and prepare us like nothing else to be the leaders He calls us to be. I have found this to be a reoccurring pattern in my life as the Lord takes me in and out of seasons of repentance. God often needs to humble those He has called, even as He calls those He has humbled.

Allow me to describe one of those times. It was unexpected on my part but necessary to continue to be used by God in the areas of leadership to which He had called me. It was undoubtedly a work of the Holy Spirit. It was nothing I could muster up, and certainly nothing that I asked for, but God knew it was needed. As a leader, I needed a heart check. Trying to be a good example to others all the time is exhausting, and God in His kindness wanted to set me free from myself.

It lasted almost two weeks. The Holy Spirit was relentless in His work of conviction and very thorough. Throughout the day, memory after memory was brought to my mind. Some things were from childhood, others were much more recent. All of them were seemingly innocent events that God reminded me of and then showed me the truth of what they looked like from His perspective. He went deeper, exposing selfish motives, hateful words I had spoken, secret intents that prompted me, competitive attitudes with friends, vengeful thoughts I delighted in. Things I had been proud of and thought "award worthy" were not hidden from the light of truth. He showed how even those things were ruined by my sin.

I was shocked. I was laid low. I was sick to my stomach with disgust. I couldn't stop shedding tears of regret. I was horrified to discover that I was sinful to the core and never knew it. And, even worse, I couldn't do anything to fix it. I could see how all of my attempts to be good, always doing the right thing, were all sinful as well. They were sinful because in my heart, I thought I could actually be good enough on my own merit. I thought that somehow by my behavior I could impress God and earn His favor. Even my attempts at humility were laced with pride. The Holy Spirit revealed to me in my spirit what I truly thought: *God, You got a pretty good deal when I "signed up" to follow You. Won't I be a wonderful addition to Your team?* Oh, I am ashamed at how wrong I was. The exact opposite was true. I was anything but suitable to belong to Him.

It felt like I was being crushed, cut to the core underneath the all-seeing eye of a perfect, righteous God Who hated sin. There was no escape. No safety of comparing myself with someone more sinful than me. That wasn't an option. It was just God's holiness face to face with my worthlessness. The comparisons were glaringly obvious. I had never seen myself with such holy clarity before and I was grieved with what I saw. With every sin He brought to light, I would repent, and repent, and then repent some more...there was nothing else to do. I pleaded with Him to take away my sin. I didn't want it anymore. I hated it and wanted nothing to do with it. And then when it felt like I couldn't bare it anymore, when I thought that I would be in this place forever...He took it all away. The Holy Spirit's deep work of conviction ceased and I could breathe again. All that was left was this truth: Jesus forgave me.

"Then one of the seraphim flew to me with a live coal in his hand, which he had taken with tongs from the altar. With it he touched my mouth and said, 'See, this has touched your lips; your guilt is taken away and your sin atoned for.'" (Isaiah 6:6-7)

Isaiah knew what it was like to be completely unacceptable, sinful to the core, and thoroughly unclean. In the light of his vision of God on the Throne, the clarity of God was a picture of holiness, righteousness, and perfection. He felt the unbearable pain of conviction and the realization that he was a dead man because of it. He was powerless to save himself and that is when we see the divine intervention. To be touched by the hot coal that was taken from the altar was painful, but it was a pain that led to life. Oh the relief! Truly blessed is the man that the Lord does not hold his sins against him. Oh to be clean again!

And that is why I tell you that when the Lord showed me my sin, it was one of the best gifts He could ever give me. You see, I was grateful for His forgiveness *before* this season but I didn't really know HOW MUCH He had to forgive me for. It is like what Jesus said about the woman whom the Pharisees judged when she worshiped Him by anointing His feet with oil and washing His feet with her tears: *"Therefore I tell you, her sins, which are many, are forgiven—for she loved much. But he who is forgiven little, loves little"* (Luke 7:47).

The result of knowing your sins are forgiven is pure gratitude. Less striving, more laughter. Less watching my back, more loving on Him. Less eyes on me and my behavior, more of my eyes on Him and His work on the cross. Less critiquing others, more grace offered. Let me tell you, friends, I LOVE HIM! No one else would ever have done this for me. No one else could, just Him, just my Jesus. *"Then I heard the voice of the Lord saying,*

'Whom shall I send? And who will go for us?' And I said, 'Here am I. Send me!'" (Isaiah 6:8).

ME!!!! Pick me! Pick me! Gratitude changes us. When you should be dead and you get a second chance on life, it puts things into perspective. Isaiah, the unclean (now made clean) man is immediately called into leadership. No training necessary because he had seen the Lord God and lived to tell about it. Sometimes leaders are called simply to go and tell their story. Leaders, go and tell others what the Lord has done for you.

Jesus, the True and Better Isaiah
Just like Isaiah, Jesus was willing to be sent by God into our world to live among a people of unclean lips. He took on our sin and felt the utter shame of it, being separated from a holy God. Even though He never sinned, He felt the pain, shame, and weight of it. He personally knows what it feels like to be us. And because He felt the FULL weight of our sins, stood face to face with the holy, righteous God, and became the sacrifice, you and I are granted pardon. Jesus is the true and better coal that touched our lips and took away our sin. Forgiven. Exonerated. Set free. We are released from the bondage and pain of sin so that we may live for Him with purpose, passion, and value.

Craig's Response
We are all unclean leaders who serve a holy God. Like Isaiah, Joshua the high priest in Zechariah 3 is someone I completely identify with who was clothed in filthy garments before a holy God. I feel the stinging accusations of Satan who declares that I am not worthy of being in God's presence. But then I hear the compassionate voice of the Savior standing next to me, as He rebukes Satan because He has chosen me and plucked me from the fire. And then with unspeakable joy, I read the words, *"Remove the filthy garments from him. Behold, I have taken your iniquity away from you and I will clothe you with pure vestments"* (Zechariah 3:4). As I heard long ago from Tim Keller, "We are more sinful and flawed in ourselves then we ever dared

believe, yet at the very same time we are more loved and accepted in Jesus Christ then we ever dared hope."[21]

My friends, this is the good news of the gospel. In spite of our guilt, we have a God Who forgives our sin, removes our filth, and then chooses to use us for His glory. The Lord is still asking, *"Whom shall I send, and who will go for us?"* (Isaiah 6:8). He is not looking for perfectly clean people who desire position, privilege, or power. Rather, He is looking for imperfect people who are typically reluctant to the limelight. And in His search, the Lord is looking for people, like Isaiah, who in spite of being unclean willingly say, *"Here am I. Send me!"*

Chapter Twelve
The Unsatisfied Leader: The Woman at the Well
Craig Trierweiler

"Sir, give me this water, so that I will not be thirsty or have to come here to draw water."
John 4:15

The Empty Man
I recently attended a training event equipping Christians to share their story of salvation in three minutes or less in a way that compels a person to treasure Christ. In simple terms, it is ordinary people testifying about an extraordinary God. It is something every one of us should be able to do because each of us has a story of transformation that God has done. There are no bad testimonies! Our salvation story is awesome not just because of what God saved us OUT of, but what He saved us FROM!

My three minute testimony is a version of an empty bucket. During my teenage years, no matter what I tried to satisfy my life with, it was like a bucket with holes leaking out the bottom. I was chasing the wind but couldn't capture even a handful of satisfaction or joy. I drank alcohol, but it left me empty. I dated girls, but it left me lonely. The best way to describe my teenage years is: **W.A.S.T.E.D.**

Weary

Aimless

Shameful

Timid

Empty

Depressed

Then in February of 1993, at 16 years old, I met this man named Jesus. His love for me, expressed through His death on the cross, captivated me and began to plug the leaks in my bucket. I took hold of Him because He took hold of me! From that moment, transformation began to occur. He gave me rest for my weariness, direction for my aimlessness, acceptance for my shame, boldness for my timidity, fullness for my emptiness, and joy for my depression. This extraordinary God took a WASTED kid and began to FILL me up. He took an unsatisfied teenager with a bucket full of holes, and began to plug the leaks and satisfy my longings.

The WASTED Woman

There is a woman in the Bible whose name is unknown to us. She is known simply as the "Samaritan woman" or the "woman at the well" (John 4). Prior to meeting Jesus, her life was a train wreck of shame, rejection, and empty pursuits. Like me at 16, she was WASTED. After she encountered Jesus, she testified about the awesome power of God, who meets our deepest longings and fills our deepest needs. And the turning point of this woman's life happened on an ordinary day when she was not expecting to encounter the God of the universe. Yet, on that day, this woman, whose bucket was full of holes, was face to face with Jesus Who offered living water. As she walked up to the well to meet Jesus, this woman was WASTED:

> **Weary -** She is weary from a life of being used by men. She is weary of chasing the wind but finding nothing to fulfill her. She is so weary she eventually asks Jesus to give her water *"so that I will not be thirsty or have to come here to draw water" (v. 15)*. This woman simply wants a

life of peace and rest, but all she has is exhaustion. Such a life describes a good number of people who are so weary of the rat race that they are pursuing anything that will give them satisfaction.

Aimless - She has a wandering eye and aimless pursuits. She is probably known in town as an adulterer, and one who wanders from man to man looking to be satisfied. But nobody she was with ever satisfied her deeper craving. About the only thing consistent in her life is her regular trip to the public well where she collected water for the day. But there is nothing in life that gives her purpose or meaning. She is aimless and wandering for the next best thrill.

Shameful - Jesus knows everything about her shameful past. She's had five husbands in her lifetime! That's a lot of marriages even in our culture. But in the first century, five marriages would be a laughable amount. Not only that, she is living with another man who is not her husband. Reading between the lines, this woman has dealt with a life of shame and has experienced a long, moldy bread trail of rejection. The men who married her probably used her. And somewhere along the way, this woman has turned bitter, sour, and carries an identity of shame.

Timid - With all of her experiences, how can she trust anyone? When men look at her, she feels undressed. When women look at her, she feels mocked. She has grown timid and afraid. So, when she meets Jesus at the well, it is not only a breach of social custom, it also hits right to the heart of her timidity and fear. When Jesus asks her for a drink, she likely wonders what His play is. She asks, *"How is it that you, a Jew, ask for a drink from me, a woman of Samaria? (For Jews have no dealings with Samaritans)"* (v. 9). Maybe it's a hint of sarcasm, or her protective outer shell that doesn't want to get hurt again.

Whatever it is, this woman is closed up and self-protective.

Empty - The woman may have walked every day to fill up her skins of water, but her own heart was empty and leaking. She was deeply unsatisfied with life. Her life was a trail of tears. No matter what she tried to fill her bucket with, by the time she got home, her skin was empty again. Sex brought temporal pleasure, but no permanent satisfaction. Marriage didn't work because she never felt safe or protected. Friendships with women who loved her were probably nonexistent. Her relational network is a train wreck of divorces and broken hearts.

Depressed - *"Where do you get this living water?...Sir, give me this water"* (v. 11, 15). Wouldn't you be depressed if you're whole life was spent in a little town and your reputation was ruined beyond hope? This woman lived in a glass house that didn't hide an ounce of her indiscretions. Her past haunted her. Her present rejected her. Her future daunted her. Whatever "living water" Jesus offered sounds like it could fill her up and meet the darkest points of her depression.

From WASTED to FILLED
This ordinary woman meets an extraordinary God and her life is transformed. Up until this moment with Jesus, she has been an unsatisfied woman. Now because of Jesus, she is changed forever. Her weariness has been given hope. Her aimless life has been given purpose. Her shameful past has been forgiven. Her timidity has changed to boldness. Her emptiness has been filled. Her depression has changed to joy. Do you believe God still does this today?

With that transformed life, this ordinary woman takes the news of an extraordinary Jesus back to her town and begins to testify to people about the living water. Imagine the shock and awe of people who know this woman's past! She used to hide her face and dart her eyes away from people, ashamed of who she was. Now her eyes beam with excitement and she radiates with joy! Her bucket is full and she is spilling her testimony to everyone who will listen.

Here is one of the coolest lines in the story: *"Many Samaritans from that town believed in him because of the woman's testimony"* (John 4:29). Wow! No Bible training. No discipleship seminar. No doctoral degree. Just an unsatisfied woman who met an extraordinary God and went from wasted to filled! And as a result of her changed life, she became a leader to her people. It reminds me of our neighbor when I grew up as a kid. Linda loved Jesus and befriended my mom for the sole purpose of winning her to the Lord. Linda had no Bible training or special schooling, but she had a relationship with Jesus that was contagious. In time, not only did my mom come to trust Jesus, but our entire family also came to faith. Praise God for leaders like Linda who use their sphere of influence to reach their neighborhoods for Jesus.

The woman at the well likely had no desire to be a leader, yet she was God's instrument to reach her town with the good news of Jesus. This woman had a past that many would think made her unqualified, but by God's grace she was used to reach family, friends, and neighbors. She did not have a position or hold an office of power. But equipped with a testimony of a changed life, this woman became a powerful influence in the hands of God. She went from WASTED to FILLED, and with that story she wanted everyone to know about the man called Jesus.

One of the great things about God is that He is in relentless pursuit of ordinary, reluctant leaders who will boldly testify of the transformation God has done in their life. What is your story of grace? If you had to summarize the transforming work of God in your life, how would you say it? In other words, if you had 30 seconds to share your story with a person in an elevator, how would you capture people with the good news of the Savior?

Jesus, the True and Better Samaritan Woman

Consider the life of Jesus, from a true and better perspective. My teen years were WASTED, just like the life of the Samaritan woman. But, consider Jesus:

> **Weary** - Jesus arrived at the well that day *"wearied from the journey."* And certainly His 33 years of life led Him *wearied* to the cross, where He poured out every last ounce of energy in order to save His people.

> **Aimless** - Not one day of Jesus' life was spent wandering or without purpose. His every step was meaningful. Luke 9:51 says, *"When the days drew near for him to be taken up, he set his face to go to Jerusalem."* He resolutely set His face. He was determined. He was tempted in every way, just as we are, yet He lived His life with purpose and focus that was unparalleled.

> **Shameful** - Jesus never committed one shameful action. However, as He hung on the cross, the shame of the world was being placed upon His shoulders. In that moment, Hebrews 12:2 says that *"for the joy that was set before him endured the cross, despising the shame, and is seated at the right hand of the throne of God."* The song by Chris Tomlin says it well: *"You took our sin; You bore our shame; You rose to life; You defeated the grave; And a love like this, the world has never known."* [22]

> **Timid** - Jesus was not a timid man. Meek, yes. But not timid. He spoke with authority. The people marveled at His teaching. And because of His extraordinary boldness, He was contagious, giving people courage who were formerly timid. Somehow, this Samaritan woman with a shameful past became the town evangelist because she encountered Jesus and was set free!

Empty - Jesus was the fullest man who ever walked the earth. But, in His final night before the crucifixion, He too was emptied and poured out. Luke 22 records His cries of agony as His sweat was like drops of blood falling to the ground: *"Father, if you are willing, remove this cup from me. Nevertheless, not my will, but yours, be done"* (v. 42). In a remarkable paradox, Jesus was emptying himself so that all who believe in Him may be filled up to overflowing!

Depressed - There is no record of Jesus smiling or laughing in the Bible. But we must assume He did. Could there have been a more joyful man to ever live? When He tells a parable about people entering heaven, He says they will receive this welcome: *"Enter into the joy of your master"* (Matthew 25:23). This extraordinary God is still able to turn the darkness of depression into the light of pure joy. He is able to transform curmudgeons by placing a crown of delight upon their head.

Are you an Unsatisfied Leader?

I know that some who read this feel disqualified because of your past. Like the woman at the well, you may have wasted years of life in patterns of sin. Perhaps you have a reputation in your community that is tainted by a lack of integrity, bad choices, and sexual dysfunction. Perhaps those who know you best would define you by the corrupt decisions and broken relationships that litter your past. As for the future, maybe nobody expects you to be a leader or an influencer of people. But the beauty of the gospel is that God often transforms reluctant leaders and equips them with a powerful testimony to influence friends and family with the good news of the gospel.

You do not need a title, position, or public office to influence people. All you need is the testimony of a changed life that showcases the grace of God. Imagine the impact you could have attending a family reunion and testifying that God has transformed your WASTED life and FILLED it with hope.

Imagine gathering at a class reunion with friends who knew you in high school for your promiscuity but you are able to testify about the promises of God. Like the woman at the well, God often sends us back to friends and family to testify about a God Who can change our lives from a mess to a miracle.

For the last two decades, I have had the joy of ministering the gospel in the same town I grew up in. Like the woman at the well, I have encountered people from high school who knew me during my wasted years of youth. Likewise, I have met others from high school who have also been transformed by the gospel of Jesus. It is a powerful testimony when Jesus gets hold of a wasted life and fills it up with His all-satisfying love. Never underestimate what God can do with the power of one changed life.

During my WASTED teenage years where I was unsatisfied and empty, the church we attended would sing a song that still reverberates in my head. The verses of the song were an anthem to the woman at the well who was transformed by the grace of Jesus.

"Fill My Cup, Lord."
Like the woman at the well, I was seeking
For things that could not satisfy.
And then I heard my Savior speaking –
"Draw from My well that never shall run dry."

Fill my cup, Lord;
I lift it up, Lord;
Come and quench this thirsting of my soul.
Bread of Heaven, feed me till I want no more.
Fill my cup, fill it up and make me whole.[23]

- Are you weary? Ask the Lord to give you rest and drink from His satisfying water.

- Are you aimless? Ask the extraordinary God to touch your ordinary life and give you a new purpose and direction to serve Him.

- Are you full of shame? Maybe the past haunts you, your present rejects you, and your future daunts you. Ask Him to reshape your new identity as a child of the Most High God.

- Are you timid? Ask for boldness. God did not give you a spirit of fear. Once the extraordinary God touches your life, you will be changed, and you too can learn to tell your story in a way that is clear and compelling.

- Are you empty? Pray that the Lord will plug the leaks in your life, change the pursuits of your heart, and begin to fill you with His satisfying love.

- Are you depressed? Ask the Lord for joy in the darkness. If you find yourself in an endless cycle of going back and forth to the well and there is no end to the madness, turn to the One who has living water and say, "Sir, give me this water."

Kori's Response
Our honeymoon had been a short stop in Branson, Missouri that was picked simply because we were relocating to Michigan. So we decided we would save up and splurge for our 10th anniversary. What an experience! It was an all-inclusive, adult-only, week-long stay at a beautiful resort in Mexico . At the time, we had four kids, ranging in ages from 2 to 7, and my normal day was exhausting and intensely full of activity. The break was essential and the vacation was amazing.

I had never experienced anything like it before. It was like I stepped out of my life and into someone else's. Our days were filled with sunshine, walks on the beach, relaxing by the poolside, and reading books. Meanwhile, other people served us a limitless supply of amazing food. By the end of the week, I was re-energized, full, and happy. That is when I sensed the Lord draw me into a conversation: *"Kori, how did you like this lifestyle?"* I answered in my heart, *"Oh, Jesus, I loved it here. Thank You so much."* Then I heard another question, *"Kori, would this be enough for you, if this was all there was in life?"* In my spirit, I felt at first, *"Oh no God, even as amazing as all of this has been, this could never be enough for me. I don't know what it looks like or how to describe it, but I WANT so much MORE than this."* And that is when I heard His response, *"Kori, don't worry, My child, I have so much more for you!"*

With those words, He spoke directly to my God-given emptiness with a promise of more. Even with all the best that life has to offer here, it could never be enough because we were made for so much more than this. Just like the woman at the well, the unsatisfied leader, there is a hope that no matter who you are, how much you experience, how far you wander, or how much you accomplish—there is one, the true Leader, Who is able and willing to satisfy our deepest longings. The best is yet to come!

Chapter Thirteen
The Uneducated Leader: John
Kori Trierweiler

"Now when they saw the boldness of Peter and John, and perceived that they were uneducated, common men, they were astonished..."
Acts 4:13

Craig and I met the first week of college and soon discovered we had all the same classes. So naturally, we would sit together in class, walk together to the next one, and attempt to study together in the library. I suppose that is one of the reasons we became such good friends. Throughout the semester, I began to notice a pattern when it came time to take a test. I would study for hours, rereading the material, going over my notes from lectures, and cramming the night before the big day. Craig on the other hand, would casually take out his notes a mere ten minutes before the class, and quickly glance over them before taking the exam.

The results were, in my opinion, always unfair. He would unfailingly ace the test with flying colors and I, after all my efforts, was lucky to get a C+. Even his papers that took him a fraction of the time it took me, always came back with rave reviews from the professor, while mine were full of helpful "suggestions." I was in awe (maybe even a little bitter) of how easy education was for him and how hard it was for me.

Academics, classroom learning, writing papers, being book-smart has never been easy for me. So when God called me to lead Bible studies and write books it seemed laughable at first. And then when I found out that He was serious, it was downright terrifying.

John, the Uneducated Leader

John was a simple fishermen. One ordinary day while he was mending the nets together, something he expected to be doing for the rest of his life, the extraordinary happened. It was something that changed John's life forever. The prophet Jesus, whom everyone was talking about, came by his boat specifically to talk to him. Jesus wanted John for His very own disciple. This meant He was calling John to leave the only life he knew and come spend time with Jesus, learn His ways and become like the Rabbi. John must have sensed this was a once-in-a-lifetime significant invitation because he immediately left his father in the boat and followed Jesus. Up to this point, John had been trained and educated all these years for a career in fishing. It was all he knew. But now Jesus, the Rabbi, was calling him to come and take lessons from Him for an entirely different line of work.

What a change for young John to leave his home and go full-time on the road with Jesus and a group of disciples! It was exciting from the beginning. There were miracles, parables, and healings. Every day was a new and unexpected adventure. It was a hands-on education just being around Jesus. But I believe one of the best lessons John learned is tucked away in this passage: *"One of his disciples, whom Jesus loved, was reclining at the table at Jesus' side"* (John 13:23). The writer of these words is John himself. Out of all the disciples, John refers to himself as the disciple whom Jesus loves. And his place is at Jesus' side.

In the midst of that wild trip of following Jesus, he somehow experienced Jesus' love in a real and intimate way. He learned that he was dearly loved by Him. The KJV words it this way: *"Now there was leaning on Jesus' bosom one of his disciples, whom*

Jesus loved." John was leaning against Jesus' chest like a little child would cuddle up with a trusted big brother or father. In a room full of all the disciples, John was snuggled up at Jesus' side, unashamed of his affection, knowing he was wanted, cherished, and loved. He identified himself as the disciple whom Jesus loved and that changed everything. He was educated by love.

After Jesus' death, the religious leaders thought they had gotten rid of this disruptive no-name leader and His followers, but they were mistaken. When they heard His disciple John teaching among the crowds, it was like deja vu all over again. They thought they were through with this guy, and yet here are John and Peter speaking just like Jesus. Where did they come from? How did they know the Scriptures so well? And where did they get such eloquence, wisdom, clarity, and confidence? The similarities to Jesus were undeniable. In fact it says in Acts 4:13 that when the people *"saw the boldness of Peter and John, and perceived that they were uneducated, common men, they were astonished. And they recognized that they had been with Jesus."* John was not chosen as a young boy to be educated by the Sanhedrin, with years of learning and memorization of the Torah. He simply spent time with Jesus, allowing Jesus to love him. And Jesus' love makes ALL the difference. As John said in one of his letters, *"There is no fear in love, but perfect love casts out fear"* (1 John 4:18).

Before we started, Craig and I decided we would work on our *I Want to be a Nobody* chapters separately and when they were finished we would put them together. He, of course, completed all of his chapters in record time, while I was still struggling to complete even one. I thought perhaps I needed to hear the way he put together a chapter before I could continue, so he obliged.

While he eagerly read me one of his chapters, my heart sank. Wow, his chapter was really good, I mean REALLY good! At the time, I knew I should be excited for him and encourage him about how strong, deep, and consistent his writing was. But all I could think about was how much better he was than me. I think I missed his last paragraph entirely because an onslaught of negative thoughts hit me: *Why is writing as natural as breathing for him, when I struggle through every sentence? His chapters are so much better than mine. It would be better if he just wrote this book without me. My writing seems so elementary compared to him. What if I'm just going to hold him back? I'm so incapable and completely unnecessary here.*

Sometimes I look at myself and just despise my insecurities. There they go again beating me down, stopping me in my tracks, screaming at me to quit. *You are a nobody. You can't do anything significant.* The only thing I knew to do in that moment was to cry out to the Lord to help me from drowning in my own self-doubt. But when I reached out for help from the Lord, I heard a different spin on things: *Kori, I love it that you can't seem to handle anything on your own. It's okay with Me that you find writing hard because that is when you turn towards Me. It's the point when you seek My wisdom, My presence, My perspective. That's when you lean into Me, lay your head on My chest and let Me love you.*

It's as if God allows writing to be hard for me so that I can't plow full speed ahead without Him. I have no other option but to humble myself and plead with Him for help. And He meets me there. He loves me there. He teaches me there. I often see my weaknesses as pathetic but He looks at them and sees them differently. They are beautiful opportunities for Him to come and abide with me. With all my insecurities and desire to hide, He invites me to be tucked away in Him, buried deeply in His love, safe from harm, while He comes with His strength and ability to live life through me. And looking back now, as I write this last chapter and the words flow, Jesus and I both know that this is His working and not my doing. I am humbled and in awe of His grace towards me. Privileged and honored that He would use me. This is the way He educates me, by enveloping me in His love. This uneducated, C+ schoolgirl, who has never taken a writing class in her life, is being educated in secret by the love of Christ.

Jesus, the True and Better John

Jesus is so evident in John's life because he spent time with Him. The words that John speaks in his letters are borderline obsessive about God's love. It seems from John's perspective, it is the one and only requirement. His message is that God is love —that He loved us first before we could ever love Him or anyone else for that matter. In his letter in 1 John, John continually highlights the love of God:

> *"Beloved, let us love one another, for love is from God, and whoever loves has been born of God and knows God. Anyone who does not love does not know God, because God is love. In this the love of God was made manifest among us, that God sent his only Son into the world, so that we might live through him. And this is love, not that we have loved God but that he loved us and sent his Son to be the propitiation for our sins. Beloved, if God so loved us, we also ought to love one another."* (4:7-12)

Loving those whom God has called us to lead may be the most important thing we could possibly do for them. It is the way we show Him off to those who have never experienced Him before. Loving God and loving others is some of the best education you could ever have when it comes to leadership. Ask yourself, do I really love those whom God is calling me to lead? Ask Him to show you how. It makes all the difference in the world.

John repeatedly echoes the message of love that Jesus gave him. In John's Gospel, he records these words from Jesus:

> *"As the Father has loved me, so have I loved you. Abide in my love. If you keep my commandments, you will abide in my love, just as I have kept my Father's commandments and abide in his love."* John 15:9-10

John goes on to speak of the joy of this type of love and how it is so powerful that when we receive it, it not only transforms us but we have it in such abundance that we are able to love others with the same love with which He loves us. Oh, to be leaders who love the way that Jesus does!

Friend, if God is calling you to something and you are tempted to say, "Lord, you don't need me for this," I want you to see His loving answer: *"It's true, my disciple, I don't need you for this but I want you for this. I will help you in all areas. We will get to be together through the entire process. I love being with you. I love filling your weaknesses. I love working through you. Lean into Me and we will do this together so that I may love others through you."*

Craig's Response
The Scripture says *"knowledge puffs up while love builds up"* (1 Corinthians 8:1). It is possible to be well trained in religious education and very out of sync with Jesus. Paradoxically, it is possible to have no religious education and be very in sync with the love of Jesus. I recall officiating a wedding years ago when I was approached afterward by a group of three pastors who were well equipped with a realm of religious knowledge. They wanted to know what I believed on certain issues and began listing off terms I had never heard of. The inquisition was things like: *Did I believe in supralapsarianism or infralapsarianism?* I looked at them and responded, "I'm not sure, but I do love Jesus." They smiled, but were slightly disappointed at my lack of intellectual precision.

The good news of the gospel is that God often uses uneducated leaders to profoundly impact people for His Kingdom. God is not opposed to religious education or degrees. But more important than doctoral, master's, or bachelor's degrees is that we have a doctoral degree in loving Jesus and spending time with Him. If you are a reluctant leader who doesn't feel qualified because you are uneducated or don't know enough about the Bible, take comfort from John the Apostle and from my wife. Both of them are masters at leaning against the chest of Jesus to spend time learning from Him. That is the type of disciple Jesus is looking for.

Just today, a couple from our church sent me a prayer that displays the heart of John. In turn, I pray this for you: *"Heavenly Father, we ask that Craig **makes time with You a priority** in his* *daily routine. To step away from distractions, technology, and even his beloved family so he can have **one-on-one time with You**. Let Craig know and feel You meet him during these **intimate times**. So that he can talk to You and so he can **be still and listen** to what You have to say to him. Help Craig keep his mind focused on things above and not on earthly things.*

*We know that we are human and we can be tempted to wander. Pull him back and put his eyesight on You. Whether it's through worship, confession, or thanksgiving, have him feel assured, comforted, and overwhelmed by Your presence as **You speak straight to his heart**. We also ask that he is able to discern Your voice. To truly know that it's You. We pray that Craig is open to hear from You. Have him be **filled with Your love** and peace when You reveal your plans for him. And as Craig continues to be obedient to Your plans for his life, give him a joyful heart and the protection and strength to carry out Your mission. We pray all this in the name of Your precious Son. Amen."*

Chapter Fourteen
The Undeserving Leader: John The Baptist
Craig Trierweiler

"Therefore this joy of mine is now complete. He must increase, but I must decrease."
John 3:29-30

Check Your Ego at the Door
One of my best friends and co-laborers in ministry is our executive pastor, Rick Stewart. Rick has many sayings that have become woven into the DNA of our staff, such as "we are in the people business" and "everything effects everything." But at the top of the list is his saying, *"Check your ego at the door."* In other words, leadership is not all about us. At the root of leading other people, we must have a humility that says, "I am undeserving."

The moment we feel deserving or entitled, trouble arises. God used a very difficult season of ministry and leadership pressure in 2006 to address deep character flaws in my own heart. Most of it all came down to authority and submission. My ego was being carried with me everywhere I went. I wasn't checking my pride at the door. I wasn't laying down my rights toward those in authority. My life and my leadership were all about me and I felt I deserved better treatment. God would take me through a seasons of brokenness to fix this attitude in me.

I wonder: How many of us would be content to minister in obscurity our whole lives? How many of us would actually be content if our accomplishments were never noticed? How many of us have the humility to see other people elevated while we ourselves are demoted? There is a man in Scripture who was one of the greatest leaders of all time, yet he knew he was undeserving and thus checked his ego at the door.

John the Baptist may have been the most eccentric leader in the Bible. His wardrobe was camel's hair. His diet was locusts. His message was a thundering theme of repentance. But he gained a massive following as people recognized that God's presence was working mightily through him.

Yet, John the Baptist had checked his ego at the door. When people tried to elevate him and push him to the front stage, John was quick to exit to the backstage. When people put the spotlight on him, John kept pointing the spotlight to the Messiah who was yet to come. Look at how undeserving John felt as a leader. This saying of John was so significant, it is quoted in three Gospels:

-Matthew 3:11: *"He who is coming after me is mightier than I, whose sandals **I am not worthy to carry."***

-Luke 3:16: *"He who is mightier than I is coming, the strap of whose sandals **I am not worthy to untie."***

-John 1:26-27: *"Among you stands one you do not know, even he who comes after me, the strap of whose sandal **I am not worthy to untie."***

"I am not worthy!" That is the voice of a man who knows he does not exist for his own glory but the glory of Another who is greater than him. To strap on someone's sandals would be the most humble and lowly tasks of servanthood. Picture a shoe shiner in an airport terminal or in the underground of Grand Central Station. The person in the chair is usually the one with the money, power, and authority. The person shining the shoes is the servant. And the shoes themselves are grimy and dirty from walking through dusty streets.

Still, John the Baptist says he was so undeserving that he wasn't even worthy to untie or carry the Messiah's sandals. He pointed all the glory and attention back to the One Who deserved the credit. The Gospel of John likens John the Baptist to the moon and Jesus to the sun:

> *"There was a man sent from God, whose name was John. He came as a witness, to bear witness about the light, that all might believe through him. **He was not the light, but came to bear witness about the light**"* (John 1:6-8).

The moon, of course, has no light properties in itself. All the moon does is reflect the light of the sun. My friend, the minute we start thinking we are the sun, and not the moon, we are bound for trouble as leaders. We are moons, darkened and undeserving with no special properties of light in ourselves. But when we reflect the glorious light of Jesus, what a magnificent difference we can make in the darkness of this world!

Handling Rejection

How do you handle rejection? What happens at your heart level when people abandon you and follow another leader? How do you feel when people leave your church to follow the leader of another church? I admit, rejection has been one of the hardest things in my ministry life. It makes me feel like a failure. It hits at my ego. It compounds my shame.

Many of you have probably experienced this at a personal level. Perhaps family members who were once close to you have broken relationship with you. Perhaps close friends who once were confidants have turned away. I don't know of any greater sting to the human heart than that of feeling personally rejected. It is so significant that both King David and King Jesus are quoted in the Scripture to say the same thing: *"Even my close friend in whom I trusted, who ate my bread, has lifted his heel against me"* (Psalm 41:9 and John 13:18). Nobody likes to get kicked in the face by a friend or rejected by those who once followed us. And when it happens, it can cause us to feel like utter failures.

Craig Trierweiler

Yet, John the Baptist had this happen. At the height of his ministry, with crowds of people flocking to him, the Messiah shows up and begins His ministry. Right away, John had two disciples with him who, Scripture says, saw the Messiah and left John and *"followed Jesus"* (John 1:37). These two disciples who walked away to follow Jesus were Peter and Andrew. These are fairly important disciples who left John in order to follow another leader.

Let's see how John the Baptist handled this type of rejection as even more followers left him and started following Jesus. John's audience gets smaller, Jesus' gets bigger. John's crowds are dwindling, Jesus' crowds are swelling. John is downsizing, Jesus is upsizing. And the faithful few members of John's entourage are quite concerned about this apparent ministry failure. So they called a cabinet meeting and came to John with concerns about the ministry: *"Rabbi, he who was with you across the Jordan, to whom you bore witness—look, he is baptizing, and all are going to him"* (John 3:26-27).

What an awful thought! What terrible news! What a problem! Everyone was leaving John and going to Jesus! What about John's book sales? What about John's speaking tour? What about John's marketability as a headliner? What about John's fame? What about John's retirement account?

Well, John the Baptist reveals the heart of a man who has checked his ego at the door. In the moment when his glory was diminishing and Jesus' glory was increasing, John said, *"Therefore this joy of mine is now complete. He must increase, but I must decrease" (John 3:29-30).*

John had checked his ego at the door long before. As he saw the ministry of Jesus increase and his own decrease, he had complete joy! His ministry was not about his glory, but about the glory of Jesus Christ. John was the moon, simply reflecting the glory of his Creator. And once the sun began to shine, he was content to fade into the background as an undeserving leader,

118

not worthy to carry sandals. John had simply fulfilled his calling and done what God had asked him to do.

Jesus, the True and Better John the Baptist

Someday, all of us will be forgotten. Like the Tomb of the Unnamed Soldiers, our names will be lost in history and forgotten among the masses. It is humbling to recognize that most of our great-grandchildren will not even know our first names. No matter our position or influence in society, we are on the same trajectory as John the Baptist. We will decrease and yet God will increase. We are temporary placeholders who exist to serve the fame of Jesus Christ. And yet once Jesus comes to assume His rightful place in the driver seat, it should not disturb us at all to take the backseat to His glory.

Every leader is where they are at because of the leadership of another. And all of us one day will be replaced by another leader who will take the baton of leadership from us. And in the course of time, our names will be forgotten. But the legacy of Jesus will continue on. That is how it should be.

At my current position, I am here because of the remarkable leadership of a senior pastor, David Standfest, who had the courage and faith to start a church in 1990. In 1999, he took a risk and hired me as the church custodian. After his retirement in 2010, the baton of leadership was transferred to Bob Boeve who served as interim CEO. Apart from my family, those two men (Dave and Bob) have been the most instrumental people in my life. I am where I am today because of their leadership. In 2012, the baton of senior leadership was passed to me. And one day, I too will pass the baton to another who will preach about the compelling glory of Jesus Christ.

But all of us will be forgotten. That's a good thing. We are undeserving. Jesus is the sun, we are the moon. He must increase, we must decrease. John the Baptist died alone, beheaded in a prison because of a conflict with a political leader.

But most certainly the Lord stood with him and John received a welcome reward into eternity.

The question is: Are we willing to lead in obscurity? Are we willing to labor undeservedly even if we never gain a legacy or a following? Are we content with years of ministry only to be quickly forgotten in the wake of our absence?

In his book *The Emotionally Healthy Leader,* Peter Scazzero talks about the painful path of downward mobility after he was passing the baton of leadership to the next generation: "It was a humbling experience to allow my power to decrease...The number of messages on my phone decreased by 50 percent...I was being led where I did not want to go—into a place of vulnerability I could not control."[24] He continues, "I didn't want to embrace a path of downward mobility leading to the forgotten place of the cross...Now there was a tearing, a separation. The best words to describe this kind of emotional cutting is *bloody, excruciating, and horrific.* I thought I was going to die."[25]

What remarkable words from a man who knows what it is like to experience the pain of decreased influence. At some point in the process, Scazzero's wife told him, "People will forget you six months after you are gone." After the transition, Scazzero said, "She was wrong. Most people forgot me *before* the succession was completed!" My friends, if you are in leadership at any level, prepare yourself to one day be forgotten. It's okay, as long as Jesus is remembered!

God loves to use undeserving leaders. We are not worthy to carry Jesus' sandals, and yet He delights when ordinary people like us lift up His name. And one day in eternity, along with John the Baptist and every other forgotten leader, we will all give a speech. The speech comes from the lips of Jesus, who told a parable about people who serve their master: *"So you also, when you have done all that you were commanded, say, 'We are unworthy servants; we have only done what was our duty'"* (Luke

17:10). What a joy that will be when everyone's ego is checked at the door of eternity and in place of pride is the joyful reality of undeserved grace.

Fellow leaders, that is the essence of God's relentless pursuit of reluctant leaders. We have the joy and privilege to serve Jesus and make him famous. And one day we will stand before him with great joy and say: *"We are unworthy and undeserving; we have only done our duty."* To Jesus be all glory, honor, power, and dominion.

Kori's Response

It is inevitable that we as leaders will be forgotten by those who at one time acclaimed us, affirmed us, and told us how amazingly "anointed" we were. It's a good thing that those praises are not our reward. Our true and better reward is Jesus Christ Himself. He is the essence of everything that is wonderful, beautiful, and satisfying. He is our great and eternal reward, our true treasure, and home forever. He, unlike our season of leadership, will never fade. He will never forget us. He sees every sacrifice, every struggle, and every trial we suffered in order to be obedient to His calling. He will honor us and reward accordingly in His everlasting, unending Kingdom where His applaud for us will never die out and His standing ovation towards us will never fade away.

CONCLUSION
Craig and Kori Trierweiler

Joni Eareckson Tada once wrote,

> "God delights in handpicking people for leadership who are either stumbling bumblers or simply weak and ill equipped...He opens his arms to the weak and ungifted, the unlovely and unlikely. He opens His arms to sinners...The leaders God chooses are often more broken than strong, more damaged than whole, more troubled than secure. God's greatest leaders do not rise up from a bed of roses; they rise from beds of nails." [26]

That perspective of leadership is supported by both Scripture and personal experience. God chooses unqualified people like Moses, unworthy leaders like Peter, and undeserving leaders like John the Baptist so that He receives even greater glory.

The aim of these 14 chapters has been to encourage you, knowing that God relentlessly pursues reluctant leaders for His glory. He is not looking for perfect leaders. He is looking for people to bend the knee. He is looking for people who are:

Unqualified
Uncertain
Unprepared
Untrained
Unwilling
Unlikely
Unforeseen
Unworthy
Unexpected
Unfit
Unclean
Unsatisfied
Uneducated
Undeserving

Many of us see our lives as a mirror reflection of the biblical characters in this book. Both Kori and I identity with all 14 of these characteristics, which make us wonder why God chose us to lead. It is an encouragement to know that the great leaders of Scripture also had immeasurable weaknesses that made them reluctant to follow the Lord. For many in leadership, it may be helpful to pick out the top three traits that resonate with your heart and make them a matter of prayer and action.

- Though we feel unqualified, we are called into leadership by a God who qualifies us as ambassadors of Jesus Christ.
- Though we feel uncertain, we are called into leadership by a God who commands us to be strong and courageous because He is with us.
- Though we feel unprepared, we are called into leadership by a God who speaks to us and teaches us to hear His voice.
- Though we feel untrained, we are called into leadership by a God who sees our future and calls us mighty warriors.
- Though we feel unwilling, we are called into leadership by a God who wants us to obey Him with both knees bent in surrender.
- Though we feel unlikely, we are called into leadership by a God who has purposes and plans to accomplish through us that only He can see.
- Though we feel unforeseen, we are called into leadership by a God who has uniquely positioned us and called us to serve Him.
- Though we feel unworthy, we are called into leadership by a God who has declared us worthy because of the cleansing blood of Jesus Christ.
- Though we feel unexpected, we are called into leadership by a God who has given us position, power, and influence for such a time as this.

- Though we feel unfit, we are called into leadership by a God who uses our weaknesses as a showcase for the glorious nature of His grace.
- Though we feel unclean, we are called into leadership by a God who cleanses our sin, removes our guilt, and clothes us with His righteousness.
- Though we feel unsatisfied, we are called into leadership by a God who transforms our wasted lives and fills us with rivers of living water.
- Though we feel uneducated, we are called into leadership by a God who loves to use simple, ordinary people who spend time with Jesus.
- Though we feel undeserving, we are called into leadership by a God who delights when people check their egos at the door so that the name of Jesus increases.

Here is good news for all of us who feel like reluctant leaders: Those who view themselves as the least qualified are often the people God uses most greatly. Stefan Stern writes about a "paradox of leadership" saying, "The people most enthusiastically granted the power to lead by their peers are individuals who seem reluctant to do so."[27] I find this to be true, especially in a position where I am leading among peers, many of whom are older.

God is looking for people who are willing to be broken deeply so that He can use them greatly. Our prayer is that whatever God is calling you to do, you will do it all for His glory. After all, our entire life is not about us, but about the glory of Jesus Christ, Who loved us and gave Himself for us. To Him be the glory!

You are loved,

Craig & Kori Trierweiler

John 3:30
He must increase, but I must decrease.
John the Baptist

ACKNOWLEDGEMENTS

The beauty of acknowledgments is that we get to give applause and credit to people who helped make this book possible. The difficulty with acknowledgments is that we unintentionally may leave out very important people. Our desire is to honor all and say thank you!

Thank you to Joe and Traci Castañeda and Overboard Ministries for your friendship, generosity, faithfulness, and making the publishing of this book possible.

Thank you to Lyndsey Brown, our editor, who sharpened our writing, challenged our thinking, and made the final product far better than when it was started.

Thank you to Bob Boeve and Pastor Dave Standfest, who we dedicated this book to. Because you gave us a chance to lead, this book was made possible.

Thank you to our New Hope Community Church family. You are the main source of our sphere of influence and we pray this book blesses you.

Thank you to both sets of our parents, Vic & Donna Trierweiler and Mike & Diane Henry. Both of you set us on an early path of pursuing Jesus and loving Him deeply.

Thank you to Gary Bower who helped us with critical elements of our writing process and for being a friend who has given wisdom through challenging times.

Thank you to Mike Wittmer whose endorsement literally brought me to tears of joy. In one paragraph, Mike was able to capture and summarize the thoughts of our book in a compelling way.

Thank you to Kathey Youker and Claudia Chalker, two women who work tirelessly by my side at New Hope and whose efforts behind the scenes have been critical to this task.

Thank you to Bob Cook whose deep friendship and business expertise has helped to strengthen my life and the process of this writing.

And thank you to Jesus Christ, the Lord of creation and the Savior of sinners. Thank you for relentlessly pursuing us, overcoming our reluctance, and allowing us to lead for your glory.

WHAT IS OVERBOARD BOOKS

Overboard Books publishes quality books that are designed to assist in getting Christians overboard — out of the boat. It's the publishing arm of Overboard Ministries, whose mission is based on Matthew 14. In that chapter we find the familiar story of Jesus walking on water while His disciples were in a boat. It was the middle of the night, the water was choppy and Jesus freaked out His followers who thought He was a ghost. When they realized it was Him, Peter asked to come out to Him on the water, and he actually walked on top of the water like Jesus.

But what truly captivates me is the thought of the other eleven disciples who remained in the boat. I've often wondered how many of them questioned that move in the years to come? How many of them wished they hadn't stayed in the boat but had instead gone overboard with Peter? Overboard Ministries aims to help Christians get out of the boat and live life for Christ out on the water where He is. We hope and pray that each book published by Overboard Ministries will stir believers to jump overboard and live life all-out for God, full of joy, and free from the regret of "I wish I had…"

What we do
Overboard Ministries emerged in the Spring of 2011 as an umbrella ministry for several concepts my wife and I were developing. One of those concepts was a book ministry that would help other Christian authors get published. I experienced a lot of frustration while passing my first manuscript around. I kept getting rejection letters that were kindly written, but each echoed the same sentiment: "We love this book. If you were already a published author, we would love to publish it." They were nice letters, but that didn't make the rejection any easier or the logic less frustrating.

Out of that came the audacious idea to start our own "publishing company." I put that in quotes because I want people to know a couple of things. First of all, we're not a traditional publishing company like most people envision when they hear the name. We don't have a printing press in our garage, and we don't have a marketing team. Basically, we're a middle-man who absorbs most of the cost of publishing in order to help you get published, while making sure the majority of profits end up in your pocket, not ours.

Our desire is to keep costs to a bare minimum for each author. (As of this writing, there is only a minimal contract fee when your manuscript is accepted.) We provide resources and ideas to help authors work on marketing, while also providing the editor and graphic design artist at our expense. We subcontract out the printing, which speeds up the time it takes to move from final draft to bound book. Since we don't have much overhead we can keep our expenses low, allowing seasoned authors, or first-time authors like me, the opportunity to profit from their writing. This makes it possible for authors to publish more books while continuing in their current jobs or ministries.

Contact us
If you are interested in other books or learning about other authors from Overboard Books, please visit our website at www.overboardministries.com and click on the "Overboard Books" link. If you are an author interested in publishing with us, please visit our site and check out the "Authors" tab. There you will find a wealth of information that will help you understand the publishing process and how we might be a good fit for you. If we're not a fit for you, we'll gladly share anything we've learned that might be helpful to you as you pursue publishing through other means.

Thank you
Thanks for supporting our work and ministry. If you believe this book was helpful to you, tell someone about it! Or better yet, buy them a copy of their own! We completely depend on word-of-mouth grassroots marketing to help spread the word about Overboard Ministries and its publications. Please share our

website with others and encourage them to purchase the materials that will help them live "overboard" lives for Christ.

May God bless you as you grab the side of boat, take a deep breath…and jump onto the sea!

Joe Castaneda
Founder, Overboard Ministries

ABOUT THE AUTHORS

Kori Trierweiler is a wife, mother, and Bible teacher who resides in Traverse City, Michigan. She attended Moody Bible Institute, where she met and married her husband, Craig, who is a pastor. She loves to teach about the love of her Lord and Savior, Jesus Christ. She felt a calling by God and, quite unwillingly, began to write. She is a mighty prayer warrior in the kingdom of heaven, and prays that this book would draw you closer to Christ.

Craig Trierweiler grew up in Northern Michigan, surrounded by the beauty of lakes and orchards. After graduating from Moody Bible Institute in 1999, he joined the staff of New Hope Community Church. Over the years at New Hope, Craig served in a variety of roles until 2012 when he became Senior Pastor. He and his wife, Kori, have 4 children.

END NOTES

[1] Berkley, Mike. "The Reluctant Leader: Falling into Leadership as a Means to an End." *Medium,* 20 Apr. 2017.

[2] Brooks, David. "The Reluctant Leader." *New York Times,* 11 Sept. 2014.

[3] Brother Lawrence. *The Practice of the Presence of God.* New Kensington, Whitaker House, 1982.

[4] Tozer, AW *The Root of Righteousness.* Chicago, Moody Publishers, 2007, Ch. 39.

[5] Smith, Scotty. Introduction. *From Weakness to Strength: 8 Vulnerabilities That Can Bring Out the Best in Your Leadership,* by Sauls, Colorado Springs, David C. Cook, 2017, p. 13.

[6] Edwards, Gene. *A Tale of Three Kings: A Study in Brokenness.* Carol Stream, Tyndale, 1992.

[7] Berkley, Mike. "The Reluctant Leader: Falling into Leadership as a Means to an End." *Medium,* 20 Apr. 2017.

[8] Jones, Chris. "C.S. Lewis a Reluctant Convert and Beloved Thinker." *Chicago Tribune,* 23 May 2018.

[9] *Wonder.* Directed by Stephen Chboskey, Lionsgate, 2017

[10] Ingram, Chip. *Holy Ambition: Turning God-Shaped Dreams into Reality.* Chicago, Moody Publishers, 2010, p. 63.

[11] Allender, Dan and Tremper Longman. *The Cry of the Soul.* Colorado Springs, NavPress, 2015, pp. 146-147.

[12] Ingram, Chip. *Holy Ambition: Turning God-Shaped Dreams into Reality.* Chicago, Moody Publishers, 2010, p. 63.

[13] "God Can Use us All." *Bible.org,* 20 July 2009, www.bible.org/illustration/god-can-use-us-all.

[14] Eswine, Zach. *The Imperfect Pastor: Discovering Joy in Our Limitations Through a Daily Apprenticeship with Jesus.* Wheaton, Crossway, 2015, pp. 73-131.

[15] Eswine, Zach. *The Imperfect Pastor: Discovering Joy in Our Limitations Through a Daily Apprenticeship with Jesus.* Wheaton, Crossway, 2015, p. 124.

[16] Jethani, Skye. *Immeasurable: Reflections on the Soul of Ministry in the Age of Church, Inc.* Chicago, Moody Publishers, 2017, p. 200.

[17] Eswine, Zach. *The Imperfect Pastor: Discovering Joy in Our Limitations Through a Daily Apprenticeship with Jesus.* Wheaton, Crossway, 2015, p. 96.

[18] Eswine, Zach. *The Imperfect Pastor: Discovering Joy in Our Limitations Through a Daily Apprenticeship with Jesus.* Wheaton, Crossway, 2015, p. 104.

[19] Eswine, Zach. *The Imperfect Pastor: Discovering Joy in Our Limitations Through a Daily Apprenticeship with Jesus.* Wheaton, Crossway, 2015, p. 74.

[20] Eswine, Zach. *The Imperfect Pastor: Discovering Joy in Our Limitations Through a Daily Apprenticeship with Jesus.* Wheaton, Crossway, 2015, p. 127.

[21] Tim Keller. Redeemer Presbyterian Church. New York.

[22] Chris Tomlin. "Jesus, Son of God." *Burning Lights*, Sixsteps, 2013.

[23] Richard Blanchard. *"Fill My Cup, Lord."* 1952.

[24] Scazzero, Peter. *The Emotionally Healthy Leader: How Transforming Your Inner Life Will Deeply Transform Your Church, Team, and the World.* Grand Rapids, Zondervan, 2015, p. 293.

[25] Scazzerro, Peter. *The Emotionally Healthy Leader: How Transforming Your Inner Life Will Deeply Transform Your Church, Team, and the World.* Grand Rapids, Zondervan, 2015, p. 296.

[26] Tada, Joni Eareckson. Foreword. *Jesus Outside the Lines: A Way Forward for Those Who Are Tired of Taking Sides,* by Sauls, Carol Stream, Tyndale Publishers, 2015, pp. 9-10.

[27] Stern, Stefan. "What Makes People Follow Reluctant Leaders." *Harvard Business Review,* 30 June 2014.

Made in the USA
Monee, IL
22 March 2020

23688043R00085